I0569819

BOUNCING BACK

How Women Lose & Find Themselves in Marriage & Divorce

ELLEN HOLTZMAN

FERRY STREET PRESS

Bouncing Back: How Women Lose
& Find Themselves in Marriage & Divorce
© 2024, Ellen Holtzman. All rights reserved.

Published by Ferry Street Press

ISBN: 979-8-9898031-1-8 (paperback)
ISBN: 979-8-9898031-0-1 (eBook)

Learn more at EllenHoltzman.com

Without limiting the rights under copyright reserved above, no part of this publication may be reproduced, stored in or introduced into a retrieval system, or transmitted in any form or by any means (electronic, mechanical, photocopying, recording, or otherwise, whether now or hereafter known), without the prior written permission of both the copyright owner and the above publisher of this book, except by a reviewer who wishes to quote brief passages in connection with a review written for insertion in a magazine, newspaper, broadcast, website, blog, or other outlet in conformity with United States and International Fair Use or comparable guidelines to such copyright exceptions.

The material in this book is for informational purposes only. It is not intended to assess, diagnose, or treat any medical or mental health/concern and it is not a substitute for a psychotherapeutic relationship with a trained medical or mental health provider. If help is needed, the assistance of a professional psychotherapist or physician should be sought.

Publication managed by AuthorImprints.com

"If things aren't working out for you, and you're looking for soulmates to help you through the divorce journey of self-discovery, *Bouncing Back* is the book for you."

—Abigail Trafford, author of *Crazy Time*, *My Time*, *As Time Goes By* and *High Time*, a memoir.

"*Bouncing Back* is a tender hug of a memoir. With great compassion, Ellen Holtzman explores the psychological impacts of divorce, both in her role as a psychotherapist and in her own life. Informative, relatable, and heartening, these stories of heartbreak and transformation reveal deep emotional honesty and offer solace to anyone facing separation or living in its turmoil."

—Ashley Kalagian Blunt, bestselling author of *Dark Mode*.

"Ellen Holtzman's *Bouncing Back* is a fascinating and illuminating read … The book is beautifully written and is infused with the author's wisdom and compassion as an experienced clinical psychologist who gained insight from her own divorce. Dr. Holtzman invites us to settle into the blue 'comfy chair' in her consulting room for the privilege of accompanying her and two of her clients as they ride the wave of marital disruption and build new lives in the aftermath. Readers will be impressed and inspired by these women's strength, resilience, and renewed purpose, and will share the clients' gratitude for having had Dr. Holtzman as a therapist and role model."

—Joy Wolfe Ensor, PhD is the former president of the Michigan Psychological Association and the co-editor and contributing author of *The Ones Who Remember: Second-Generation Voices of the Holocaust*.

"*Bouncing Back* offers relatable, compelling, true, and hopeful stories about the impact of divorce on three women, one of them the author herself... The book will be especially valuable to women contemplating or going through a divorce but other readers, such as family members and therapists, will benefit from reading it as well. As a bonus, readers are likely to enjoy the book and to find it uplifting."

—**Karen Goldfinger, PhD is the author of** *Psychological Testing in Everyday Life* **and the co-author of** *Psychological Assessment and Report Writing.* **She is a psychologist in private practice in Connecticut.**

"For anyone who's wondered how therapy looks from their therapist's point of view, *Bouncing Back* will be both enlightening and reassuring. And it will be a trove of insights for anyone who's considered becoming a therapist herself. With warmth and clarity, Ellen Holtzman interweaves the story of her own divorce, and the growth it produced, with compassionate accounts of her clients' dilemmas and their resolution. A thoughtful, highly readable, and ultimately very moving work."

—**Dr. Laura de la Torre Bueno is a Boston area psychologist in private practice.**

"Ellen Holtzman does an excellent job of giving the reader a sense of these women's pain and struggles toward their healing and growth. The explanations of her therapeutic work are clear and informative. *Bouncing Back* would offer hope to others going through the traumatic experience of divorce and betrayal."

—**Elizabeth Owen, Psy. D. is a psychologist in private practice.**

TABLE OF CONTENTS

AUTHOR'S NOTE

This is a story of self-discovery. It follows the lives of three women in psychotherapy, struggling to define who they will become if their marriages end. Two of the women were my psychotherapy patients. As their therapist, I observed their shifting sense of self during the many months of treatment. Both patients gave me written permission to recount their experiences. I have changed their names and specific details to protect their privacy, but my portrayals stick closely to the events they described.

The third woman is me. I tell the story of the dissolution of my own marriage through the lens of an experienced therapist, exploring the changes in my identity, just as I did for the two patients I treated.

Some of the characters in my book are composites, and I have altered the chronology of certain events to create a clearer narrative. The dialogue is not a word-for-word reproduction of conversations, but an honest reconstruction of what was covered in various exchanges. My aim has been to capture the emotional truth of my life and that of my patients.

CHAPTER 1

LISA

"My husband is having an affair," Lisa said. She was a well-dressed woman in her late forties, sitting across from me in a blue easy chair that many of my psychotherapy patients called the comfy chair. She leaned forward and perched herself on the seat's edge. Her bottom lip quivered, and her cheeks looked hollowed out. Her eyes captured my attention most of all: round, wide open, and encircled by dark rings. They looked shot through with shock and grief, reminding me of my own, many years earlier.

Lisa tried to speak, but tears ran down her cheeks. "I'm sorry," she said, her voice hoarse from crying. "I feel so betrayed."

"Nothing to be sorry about," I said.

She plucked a tissue from the box, dried her eyes, blew her nose, and slumped back against the chair.

As I sat across from Lisa, I ran my fingers through my short hair and looked down at my clothes: navy cotton jacket, white blouse, and plain black slacks. The understated outfit matched the most recent iteration of myself, a competent psychotherapist.

The fingers on my right hand twitched. It was a muscle memory, and I was suddenly time-traveling backward over three decades. My husband had just left me. *I* was the patient sitting across from a therapist, pulling a tissue out of the box to wipe the tears away. I was thirty-two years old and sat with my head in my hands, sobbing.

"Any woman in your shoes would be crying," I said. I blinked a few times, pushing the grief-stricken, younger version of myself back into a dark corner of my mind where I wanted her to stay.

My brain shifted back into psychotherapist mode, and I imagined how therapy with Lisa might unfold. I hoped the parallels between our experiences would deepen the connection, making treatment more effective as a result. Although after thirty years as a psychotherapist, I realized there were no guarantees; I couldn't control the outcome of therapy.

Lisa pulled another tissue out of the box, wiping away the tears trickling down her cheeks.

"Just tell me a *little* bit about what's going on," I said in my soft, calm tone. "There's nothing to be scared of."

Lisa was quiet for a minute, composing herself. I watched her smooth her long brown hair streaked with blonde and tug at the hem of her bright purple skirt. The contrast between her sad eyes and attractive appearance stood out for me: a woman who looked her best even when she was falling apart.

"I just kicked my husband out of the house for the fourth time," she said. "It all started six months ago. I discovered he had slept with a female coworker. Greg, my husband, swore it didn't mean anything. He had sex with her one time. At least, that's what he told me. I made him leave, and he went to stay in a hotel."

She stopped talking and turned her face toward the large window in my office. Bright sunlight streamed in on this hot July day. My gaze followed hers until we were both looking at the tall tree with its deep green summer leaves on the other side of the glass pane. The tree gave my office a sense of being part of nature, even though the building was close to a busy main street in a Boston suburb. I looked around at the light blue carpet covering the office floor and at the walls painted ivory, my version of Caribbean beach colors I hoped my patients found peaceful. The white noise machine purred in the background.

I sat back in my chair and folded my hands in my lap, breathing slowly and evenly like a calm meditation teacher. Through my years as a therapist, I learned to use my posture, my hands, and even the tilt of my head to convey a message to my patients. Today my body language said, "I'm not in a rush. Just take your time."

Lisa remained quiet for a minute. Finally, she opened her mouth to speak and tears filled her eyes. I said nothing, shifting my face toward the floor. My goal was to strike the delicate balance between giving her the privacy to weep and letting her know I was ready to listen when she was ready to talk. She sighed and shook her head, picking up her story where she had left off.

"When Greg called me the next morning, he said this woman meant nothing to him. So, I told him to come back. I would give him another chance."

Everything seemed fine for a couple of weeks until one night Greg came home from work late. He told her it was a busy time of year. After several arguments, he admitted taking this other woman out for drinks after work. Lisa suspected the woman meant more to her husband than he had let on, and she made Greg return to the hotel for another week. He called her every day, telling her he knew he had made a mistake. He begged her to let him come home until she finally relented.

Why did Lisa continue to trust her dishonest husband? The question nagged at me, but it wasn't the time to ask. Right now, Lisa needed me to listen to her story without interruption.

Greg stuck to his promise a little longer this time, coming home right after work, taking Lisa out for weekend dates. Then, one Tuesday night, he didn't come home on time. When Lisa confronted him, he said he had been talking to this woman about work and had lost track of the hour; it was completely innocent. Lisa felt like she was losing her mind, unable to know if Greg was telling the truth or lying.

"Feeling crazy is one of the worst parts of this," I told her, remembering Nora Ephron's thinly veiled fiction, *Heartburn*, about her husband's affair, which I read during the terrible first year after my husband left me. The discovery that your marriage is entirely unlike what you believed it to be makes you feel as if you are losing your mind, Ephron wrote.

Greg was back in the hotel once again.

"Maybe I had overreacted," she said. "So, the next morning, I told him to come home."

Within a few weeks, Lisa discovered a text message on Greg's phone full of sexual innuendos. She had no doubt he was still carrying on with his "girlfriend," as Lisa referred to her now. She made him pack his bags and move back into the hotel. Once again, he called, texted, and begged her to let him come home.

"Greg made one promise after another," Lisa said. He would break off this affair. He was done with the other woman. Lisa was the only woman for him. "I'm almost fifty years old; we've been married for thirty years," she said. "I can't believe I am in this situation. I thought he would always take care of me. How could he have done this?"

"I know how scared you must be," I said.

"I don't know if I should let Greg come home again," she said. She teared up and stared at me, waiting for me to say something. I imagined telling her what I really thought. *Get rid of this guy immediately before he hurts you again.* But patients don't want to feel pushed. If they feel cornered or confronted, they sometimes cancel their appointment or fail to show up.

I glanced at my clock. Her story had so gripped me I'd lost track of the time. There were only five minutes left in the session. Nonetheless, Lisa seemed to expect her first appointment would help her decide what to do about her husband. Why the rush? Because it suited Greg?

"You can take your time to make a decision," I said. "Greg is living in a hotel, not on the street." Finally, I got the smile from Lisa I wanted. She leaned back in the chair and took a deep breath. Humor often worked to ease the tension in therapy.

"I hate to do this," I said. "I know this is a bad place to stop. Unfortunately, we have run out of time. Let's make an appointment for next week."

———

I looked forward to Lisa's second appointment; one of the many pleasures of my work as a therapist is hearing the next episode of a compelling story. I made this discovery a few months into my graduate training. By then, I had given up my career as a college history professor, realizing I had no choice but to bury my old life and start all over again.

"How did this week go?" I asked Lisa when she sat down in my office. She looked as well put together as she had the previous week. This time she had draped a red silk scarf around her neck.

"Greg slept at the hotel. He still calls me every day asking when he can come home. I told him I don't know." She inched forward in her chair until she sat right on the edge. The air felt charged. I watched her eyes dart back and forth. Until now, Lisa had let her husband call the shots. I wondered what it would take for her to disregard Greg's opinion, making a decision that suited her, not him. She fidgeted in her seat and twirled a long strand of hair around her finger.

I decided to lower the moment's intensity by shifting gears and asking her a question unrelated to the problem she wanted to solve. "Let's slow down a little bit," I said. "Before you decide what to do about Greg, let me get to know you better. Tell me about your background."

Lisa didn't know where to begin.

"How did you meet Greg?" I asked.

They had met in English class during their senior year of high school. She was shy and quiet, while Greg was outgoing and popular. "I was flattered he wanted to go out with me," she said. They had a good time together and fell in love.

"I married when I was only twenty," she said.

"Twenty is pretty young."

I thought about my own marriage at twenty-four. Once I became a therapist, I noticed a trend among women like Lisa and me. We married young, afraid of being alone, searching for a man to take care of us. Only years later did the pitfalls of an early marriage become clear: we hadn't given ourselves a chance to explore who we were.

"No college?" I asked.

"My parents were busy getting a divorce when I was a teenager. Nobody pushed me to go." She had briefly worked as a secretary until her first child, a daughter, was born, the second year of her marriage. Then she had two more sons. She delayed going to work until they were teenagers, when she got a job as a teacher's aide in one of the local elementary schools.

"How old are your kids?" I asked.

"They're twenty-eight, twenty-four, and twenty," she said. "The oldest bought a condo and lives by herself. The other two still live with us." Her cheeks grew soft as she talked about her kids. They were the light of her life. I wondered if she had encouraged them to marry later than she did, since all three of them remained single.

"I don't really want to get a divorce," she said. "Partly because of the kids." Many men and women have told me they don't want to end their marriage because of the pain it would cause their youngsters. Lisa's kids were grown and old enough to understand their parents' marriage was in trouble, however. I was surprised she would think it would be a problem for them if she and Greg divorced.

Lisa stopped talking. She wiped the tears away with the balled-up tissue in her hand. I could tell she wanted to bring the conversation back to Greg. He had called her the previous night, imploring her to give him another chance, but she didn't know what to do. I studied her as she spoke. Her eyes were wide, like a deer in the headlights. The word "paralyzed" came into my mind. I knew she was waiting for me to advise her. Should she let Greg come home or make him stay in the hotel? "Let's talk about the pros and cons here," I said.

Over the years, quite a few patients have described me as impartial or objective. I wouldn't go that far. I often form opinions about what people should do. My job is to keep these thoughts to myself, as a patient struggles to find her way to a decision that resonates with her, not me.

For the next fifteen minutes, Lisa vacillated. If Greg came home, at least she would know where he was and what he was doing. But Lisa was so upset with him she didn't really want him at home. If he were late returning from work, she would be staring at the clock, worrying he was having a drink with this other woman. It made her crazy to think about living like that. Perhaps it would be better if Greg stayed at the hotel. Then again, maybe this wasn't the best solution. If he moved back, he might give up his girlfriend.

I listened to Lisa go back and forth, knowing an outsider might doubt she was making any progress. However, I had done this work long enough to accept that this is how therapy began. A patient zigzagged left and then right. She backtracked, made a U-turn and went in the opposite direction. All of this was part of her process as she explored her mind.

Lisa slouched back in the chair. "I don't know what to do," she said.

"It's a big decision," I said. "You should take your time."

———————

When I closed the door behind Lisa at the end of the session, the air-conditioner kicked in with the whooshy sound it always made. In a few minutes, my office would feel like a refrigerator. I pushed open my big window. A warm breeze blew in, rustling the leaves on the tree outside.

My schedule for the day was full; even before I squeezed Lisa in for her second appointment, I had seven patients booked. In my ten-minute break, I took out the small white container with leftover Chinese food. The rich scent of beef with broccoli made my mouth water. I slipped off my shoes, curled up on the chair, and dug in.

Lisa, however, remained on my mind.

Despite being almost fifty years old, she seemed more like a girl eager to please others than a grown woman. I imagined her as the high school student she was when she first met Greg. He was the big man on campus; she was the quiet, young girl who stared at boys in the school cafeteria, too timid to talk to them.

When I added twenty years to her birth date, I realized she married in 1986. Women's lives had changed dramatically between the year she was born and the year she married. White women's participation in the labor force had increased. The number of women graduating college had more than doubled. Yet these trends appeared to have passed Lisa by.

Her background, including social class, was a factor here; no one in her family appeared to have encouraged her to go to college and get a professional job. Her life resembled a woman who came of age decades earlier, marrying young without any higher education and with limited employment prospects. What did Lisa know about herself when she got married at twenty? What did I know about myself when I got married at twenty-four? Very little, although it took me many years to admit it.

Lisa was looking at a possible future alone. Greg wouldn't be there to depend on, and she had always counted on him to take care of her. For the first time in her life she would have to pay her own bills, figure out what to do when the basement flooded, shovel the snow. When I put her dilemma this way, I understood why she gave her husband so many chances. *Scared* was the first word that came to mind, even though I could see it wasn't strong enough. A desperate, panicky feeling lurked at the edge of her consciousness, threatening to engulf her whenever she tried to imagine a future without her husband. Terror was a far better word.

Suddenly, I saw myself kneeling on the bathroom floor and gagging over the toilet bowl decades earlier. Yes, terror was the right word.

CHAPTER 2

ELLEN

Nothing seemed out of the ordinary that night. Tom, my husband of seven years, and I had already decided on our favorite Chinese restaurant for dinner. He was in the bedroom of our apartment changing when I got home from work.

"Hi," he said, taking off his sports jacket and hanging it in the closet. He picked up a comb and ran it through his dark brown hair. It looked so tidy and professional, certainly much shorter than in the photo of our wedding day on top of the bureau.

Tom loosened his tie and leaned towards the mirror, raising his upper eyelid with his finger. He popped out one of his contact lenses, blinked a few times, and slid it back in. When Tom got contacts the previous August, I was surprised. Both of us had relied on glasses since we were kids. He wore the thick Coke bottle kind and must have disliked them more than I knew, although he never mentioned it to me. Six months later, I was still getting used to the contact lenses and his recent interest in his appearance.

The contact lenses were part of Tom's new look, coinciding with the college teaching position in math he had started six months before. At the time, I assumed he wanted to make a good impression at his new job. Perhaps that's why he bought a copy of Dale Carnegie's book *How to Win Friends and Influence People* and flipped through it every night before falling asleep.

Whatever fears he had about the job, Tom kept them to himself. When I asked him how he felt about his new position, he answered with his usual one-word reply: fine. Even so he fiddled with his tie and jiggled his leg up and down. "Really?" I said. He just yawned, a signal he was done talking and didn't want to answer any more questions, leaving me in the dark about what was going on inside him.

Whenever Tom disappointed me, I made myself think about why I fell in love with him. He wasn't pushy or bossy, even if he wasn't as open as I wished. Plus he was generous and always wanted to help people. No marriage was perfect. Accepting Tom's limitations and concentrating on his positive attributes seemed to be the way to have a happy marriage and a sign of my maturity. It was only after everything changed I wondered whether my determination to appreciate Tom had led me to compromises I shouldn't have made.

———

Tom's new job was at a college in Maine, three hours from our home in a Boston suburb. Because of the long commute, he rented a room from another professor a few nights a week. Every Monday, he woke up at 5 am, kissed me goodbye, poured some steaming coffee into a thermos, and drove to Maine. After class on Thursday afternoon, he returned to our apartment. He had accepted this new position the same month I began my temporary job teaching history at Boston College. We had a "commuter marriage" like many academic couples.

Since Tom's job took him away from home a few days each week, I tried to make his first night back, as tonight was, a special occasion with a meal out at a restaurant. I thought about how much I had looked forward to it all day. "Ready?" I asked.

"Give me a minute."

I waited on the living room sofa. Although we were both college professors, our apartment was still filled with the old, worn pieces of furniture we had dug out from our parents' basements when we were newly married graduate students. Books lay everywhere. Even Tom's favorite piece of furniture, a shining, silver-top Iranian coffee table that his grandmother had given him, was buried under the textbooks he used to teach.

Sometimes I wished our home looked more sophisticated, more grown-up. At least our decision to have a baby was a sign of increasing maturity. We had been trying to conceive for ten months, and the entire time felt like a roller coaster. I would be excited after we had sex, hoping this was the month I would become pregnant. Then, two weeks later, like clockwork, I would get my period and deflate. All these highs and lows had left me fearing I would never have a baby. My envy of pregnant women was a sour taste on my tongue. Every time a mother wheeled her infant past me, I wanted to pick the baby up, stroke her soft, fuzzy hair and cuddle her to my chest. Tonight, I planned to ask Tom whether he thought it was time to consult a fertility doctor.

———

As soon as we walked into the Chinese restaurant, the odor of fried scallion pancakes and sesame oil made my mouth water. I slid in on one side of the booth. Tom sat on the other. We glanced at the menu and ordered our favorites: beef with broccoli and moo shu pork. Two plates of food soon competed for space on the small table. Tom heaped some meat on his plate and began to eat. I spooned the cabbage and pork stir fry onto one of the pancakes, smoothed it with the back of my spoon, and rolled it into a tight cylinder.

That was the last moment the night seemed ordinary.

"I want to talk about something," I said.

"What?" he asked.

"I'm kind of worried about not getting pregnant yet."

Relax. You're such a worrier, I expected Tom to say. Except he was frowning now, not smiling.

"Actually," he said. "I've decided I don't want to have a baby."

I slowly put the rolled-up moo shu pork back on my plate. Raucous laughter at the next table distracted me for a moment. I looked at Tom. Had I heard right? "What do you mean?" I asked.

"I've decided I don't want kids. I am glad you haven't gotten pregnant yet." Tom's voice sounded slow and smooth, as if he had told me he had decided not to buy the yellow car he had recently test-driven. Even decades later, I can flick a switch in my brain and replay this scene: I stared at him slack-jawed, my eyes opened wide. Tom smiled blandly back at me.

Despite the crowded restaurant, I felt like we were alone. I sat still, waiting for him to say something else. His lips didn't move. The smile remained frozen on his face. Maybe he was joking. Once when I was angry that he had taken me up the steepest hike on Mount Monadnock, even though he swore we were on the easiest route, Tom thought it was funny. Now I scanned his face, hoping the skin around his eyes would crinkle up the way it did when he tried to put one over on me. But his dark brown eyes stayed steady, and he turned back to the beer bottle he was about to lift up to his lips.

I speared a piece of broccoli with my fork and placed it back on my plate. Damp circles spread under my arms. I stood up, bolted for the ladies' room, kneeled over the toilet and threw up. Then I switched on the faucet and washed a slick sheen of sweat off my cheeks. As I turned to leave the bathroom, I caught a glimpse of my face in the mirror, tight and pale under the fluorescent light. I walked back to the table, sat down, and pushed a few pieces of broccoli around my plate with a chopstick. The sesame oil that had made my mouth water earlier in the evening turned my stomach.

"You're not going to eat?" Tom asked.

I shook my head.

We drove home in silence. He turned onto our street, and I looked out at the dark sky. Bright lights shone through our next-door neighbor's living-room window. Mary was brushing her little girl's hair. My eyes started to tear up. I had spent the past ten months with happy fantasies about a baby: Tom and I telling our parents we were pregnant, attending childbirth classes together, picking out a crib, selecting a name. I couldn't give up the future I had imagined for myself.

I rooted around in my brain, trying to find the right words. "I still want kids," I said.

"*You*," he said in a voice that cut like a shard of broken glass, "are always criticizing me." He pulled into our driveway. I straggled up to our apartment, stunned, and watched him stride down the hall to the bedroom without saying another word.

I tried to process what had just happened. Two hours earlier, I had been looking forward to having dinner with my husband. Now it felt as if Tom had whipped off a grinning face mask to reveal a sneering movie villain. He didn't want a child, after all, and he had left me with an impossible choice: I could have him or a kid, not both. Where did it leave me if I chose a child over my marriage? Divorced? How would I ever recover? I loved my husband. He had been my whole life. Who would I be if I wasn't married to him?

I lay down on the living room sofa as Tom rummaged around the bedroom. I heard the bureau drawer creak open. His bedside lamp made its double-click "on" sound. I kept wishing he would come out and talk to me. Maybe we could straighten everything out.

Part of me wanted to walk into the bedroom and ask Tom to talk it over, but I knew the outcome. He would turn his face away from mine, look down at his book, and act as if I wasn't even there. I had been timid all my life, and Tom's refusal to speak when angry had always frightened me. So, I'd learned it was best to avoid him when he was upset.

Unable to sleep, I thought back to the past month, searching for clues to make sense of a life that had been completely turned upside down. I tried to figure out why Tom had changed his mind about having a kid and whether I had done something to make him angry. He was so hard to read. Sure, I hadn't seen much of him since he had begun driving back and forth to Maine for his new teaching job. I could have overlooked a shift in his behavior I should have noticed.

I heard Tom turn off the reading lamp. The soft glow from the light disappeared, and the bedroom turned black.

Several days after our Chinese dinner, Tom left for his Maine teaching job without kissing me goodbye. I didn't call out the usual "See you Thursday." For most of the day, I sat on a soft, pink padded chair, rocking back and forth. I should have been grading my students' papers on the causes of World War II. Fifty of them stood in a pile next to me. Instead, I drifted from the bedroom to the living room and back again, replaying the scene from the restaurant in my mind.

On Tuesday, I woke up knowing I had to drive to Boston College, stand in front of 150 students, and deliver my World War II lecture. I got through the day and flew home right after my last class. Inside my apartment, I smacked my purse on the coffee table with a loud whack and grabbed the phone. I needed to speak to my friend Sally.

I had met Sally seven years earlier, right after Tom and I married and started graduate school in Pennsylvania. She was ten years older than me and divorced, living with Warren, her partner. The year Tom and I moved to Boston, she and Warren had also moved when she started teaching at Boston College. Sally picked up the phone on the first ring, and I filled her in on Tom's decision not to have kids. "I'm terrified my marriage is on the verge of collapsing," I said.

There was a long silence on the other end of the line, and I imagined the wheels spinning in Sally's practical brain. "Remember

when Warren and I went to a couples' counselor last year?" she
said. "We had been fighting a lot and learned to listen to one
another better through counseling. Maybe you and Tom should
try it." She gave me the therapist's name and phone number.

I thought about Sally's advice and tried to figure out what
Tom would think. He certainly didn't like to have any serious
conversations with me. Would it be any different in a therapist's
office? And, what kind of conversation did I want to have? Far
better than the ones we usually had. This whole baby debacle
had opened my eyes to a communication pattern that had left
us unable to resolve any of our difficulties. When we first married, I would pursue Tom when he was angry with me, begging
him to talk. But he always refused to speak. Seven years into our
marriage, I would feel sick as soon as Tom looked the least bit
annoyed. It was best to leave him alone.

Since Tom had dropped his bombshell about not wanting
a baby, I fantasized about having a different conversation. We
would look each other in the eye, speaking slowly and calmly as
we tried to understand one another. It was the kind of discussion
I imagined adults had in a happy marriage. I hoped Tom and I
could learn how to do this through counseling.

On Thursday night, he returned from Maine, changed his
clothes, and walked into the kitchen where I was cooking. We
made small talk: the drive back was easy, little traffic, chicken and
rice for dinner. I could have waited until after the meal, but I
needed to get it over with. I told him of Sally's suggestion about
marriage counseling. To my surprise he agreed to an appointment. Maybe he could see we needed professional help. Perhaps
there was still some hope for us. I felt elated at the possibility we

could find a solution to our problem. What I didn't realize at the time, and only understood after many years of practicing as a therapist, was that people agreed to come to therapy with their spouses for various reasons, many of which had nothing to do with improving the marriage at all.

CHAPTER 3

MEGHAN

On a beautiful June day, I flopped down on the comfy chair in my office. My noon patient had canceled earlier, and I was ready for a break. I opened my window, letting a warm breeze flutter through the curtains. On the street below, a gaggle of teenage girls giggled in unison in their high-pitched voices. School would be out next week, and they were probably excited about the upcoming summer vacation. The fine weather had put me in a good mood, too.

I had my routine down pat for a warm day like today. An hour-long break between patients gave me a chance to walk in the sunshine and swing by the Chinese restaurant to pick up my favorite lunch special. I had some patient notes to attend to before I could go out, but first I dialed in to check my voicemail. A young woman's voice on the message said her name was Meghan. She had read my profile on the *Psychology Today* therapist directory and would like to book an appointment.

Meghan was the third new patient to find me through the online directory that month. The days of getting a psychotherapist's name from a trusted doctor were ancient history. Instead, prospective patients preferred the ease of the internet: type in your zip code, click on the filters, such as the therapist's gender, age, area of specialty, and a list of providers popped up along with their pictures and profiles.

My millennial patients used the *Psychology Today* directory the most. Maybe the ease with which they searched for romance online made it natural to look for a therapist the same way. These twenty- and thirty-something men and women were a pleasure to work with, embracing therapy without any of the ambivalence I sometimes saw in my older patients. Millennials never knew a time when people viewed the need for psychotherapy as a sign of weakness. "Even Tony Soprano saw a therapist," one young man reminded me.

There was a more personal reason why I enjoyed these patients. I remembered myself at their age, torn up by my marital problems, yearning for an infant, and facing a difficult job market for academics. Adult life turned out to be much more difficult than I had imagined it would be. My millennial patients were as confused as I was about how to navigate the unexpected real-life problems of adulthood. I loved being their guide through this next stage of life, and I hoped Meghan would be another one of them.

When I phoned her back, she explained she had a problem in her marriage she didn't know how to deal with. "My husband changed his mind about having a second child."

My ears perked up, of course. I had never seen a married female patient whose problem sounded so much like the one I faced in my marriage. "What about an appointment at 10 am next Friday?"

"That's good," she said. She taught at the high school down the street, but school would be out in a few days. "I want to get going with therapy on my summer vacation when I have the time and energy to figure stuff out."

I liked her attitude. A willingness to do some serious work in therapy made my job easier. A week later, she sat across from me in the comfy chair.

Meghan was a tall woman, about thirty years old, with long blonde hair pulled back into a ponytail. She looked crisp and tidy in her pressed white blouse, blue shorts, and newish-looking, practical Teva sandals. I was taken aback. Without even being aware of it, I had expected her to appear frightened and disheveled, much like I did when Tom told me he didn't want a child. I made a mental note to be more careful about jumping to conclusions about Meghan based on my personal history.

"Why don't you start by telling me a little about what is going on," I said.

"Patrick, my husband, and I have been married for six years. Our daughter was born eighteen months ago. We planned to have two kids, and I thought we would try to get pregnant again this spring. Then in January, Patrick said we should stop at one kid."

"What do you feel about that?" I asked.

Meghan's eyes watered up. I pointed to the tissue box on the small table next to the chair. She pulled out a Kleenex and held it in her hand.

"I feel betrayed," Meghan said. "We agreed on having two kids, and now Patrick wants to change everything."

I studied Meghan's face. Instead of letting her tears come out, she pressed her lips together in a tight frown, making me realize she was a woman who was unusually cautious about revealing her feelings.

"What kind of plan did you two make about having a family?" I said.

"I remember where we were the first time we had the discussion," she said. "Eating dinner in the school cafeteria in college." It was the spring of their junior year, and they had been seeing each other for ten months. Their relationship was becoming serious. They were feeling each other out, trying to see if they had similar visions about their future. Both of them wanted children. They agreed on that. They differed on how many to have. Meghan wanted four, two of her own and two she would adopt. She had imagined this kind of family as a little girl playing with her dolls. Patrick said two were enough for him. Children were expensive, he reminded her.

"I knew he had a point," Meghan told me. "I compromised and decided a family with two kids would be okay with me."

She paused. Patients often hesitated when they were about to reveal shameful information, and I wondered if she would tell me something embarrassing. I thought of the stop-and-go silences punctuating the therapy session of the patient I had seen right before Meghan, a thirty-two-year-old woman named Jessica. She had come to me to discuss her troubled history of relationships with men. In a story about her uncle, she stopped talking so abruptly it felt like she had slammed her foot on the car brake. She shifted her eyes to the floor and opened her mouth. For a few seconds, she appeared to have lost her words. Then, in a stuttering voice, she confessed he had run his hand up and down her thigh when she was twelve.

Meghan turned out to be nothing like Jessica at all. When she paused, she was trying to collect her thoughts. She was a woman who spoke slowly and chose her words with care. "Deliberative" was the adjective that came to mind. She never raised her voice, but it always sounded clear and direct. Perhaps she cultivated this tone after many years of trying to teach complicated math concepts to a classroom of unruly teenagers.

"Even though I agreed with Patrick about having two kids, I can't go along with having one," she said. Her foot made a firm tapping sound on the floor. "I do not want my daughter to be an only child. I want her to have a sibling as I did. A sibling is really important."

A long silence followed. A picture of my husband, Tom, came into my mind, and I saw his blank face when he told me he no longer wanted a baby. Then I remembered the feeling of dread that snaked into my gut that night. The sound of Meghan grabbing another tissue brought me back to my office.

"Why did Patrick change his mind about children?" I asked, expecting she had more insight into her husband than I had into mine.

"He said bringing up kids is really hard." She raised her voice in mock surprise. "I said to Patrick, 'What did you expect? Of course it's hard.'" Both Meghan and her husband worked full-time. She was the high school advanced placement math teacher. Patrick worked in marketing. "One of us has to drop the baby off at daycare, pick her up, make dinner, give her a bath, and get her to sleep. Patrick says he is tired all the time. I am exhausted, too." Meghan blinked and looked away from the harsh sunlight streaming into my office window. Then, lowering her voice as if she were telling me a secret, she said, "I do more of the childcare and housework than Patrick does."

I sat back in my chair and folded my hands in my lap. I breathed in and out slowly, imagining my warm breath soothing Meghan. I had often tried to picture how a young woman today would react to a situation much like the one I had faced decades earlier: the heartbreak of a husband who decided he didn't want a baby.

Unable to resolve the problem, Meghan and Patrick had been seeing a marriage counselor for the past three months. However, they remained at a standstill. Patrick still didn't know if he wanted a second child. Meghan was sure she did. "We haven't made any progress in marriage counseling. I'll continue those sessions, but I decided I also need individual therapy," she said. "That's why I made an appointment with you."

I had been here before with patients and knew the treatment could go one of two ways. Sometimes, people used individual therapy to work on a problem they believed was interfering with their marriage. My patient, Paul, was this type of man. He was in his early forties, married for twelve years, with two sons. He and his wife had been in counseling for six months when he came to see me for individual therapy to learn how to understand his wife's feelings. But other people used individual therapy differently. Their goal was to decide whether or not they wanted to stay married. It remained to be seen which direction Meghan would take.

"Well, I'm going through different scenarios," she said. "I might still be young enough to leave my husband and look for a man who wants more kids. Does this really make sense? Should I wait to see if Patrick decides if he wants another child?"

At first, I wondered if Meghan was moving too quickly to end her marriage. Then I reminded myself she and Patrick had spent three months in marriage counseling without finding a solution to their problem. She had already given up her hope for a big family, going along with Patrick's preference to have only two children. An outsider might think of Meghan as cold and calculating. I admired her, however. She was clear-eyed about her options and willing to take charge of her life. I wished I had been like her when I was younger.

The two of us had reacted very differently to a similar marital problem. I was terrified when Tom told me he no longer wanted a child; Meghan hadn't panicked. What accounted for this difference? Personality was a factor, of course. While I was the shy girl sitting in the back of the high school class, praying the teacher wouldn't call on me, Meghan seemed like the kid who shot her hand up in the air, ready to answer any question the teacher asked.

It wasn't only our personalities that were different. Society had shifted, too. Before the growth of the women's movement in the 1970s, young women were expected to wait for a boy to phone, ask her out, and make all the plans for the date. Back then women were encouraged to be passive and defer to men. Meghan grew up in an era when women were pushed to take charge of their destinies, according to a Cision PR Newswire study. She appeared to be doing just that.

Toward the end of the hour, Meghan circled back to her husband's statement about how hard it was to raise a child. A look of irritation crossed her face. "Between taking care of our daughter and the house, I do much more than Patrick does," she said. "Sometimes Patrick admits to the marriage counselor he should do more around the house. He never does though. Whether or not we have a second kid, I would feel happier if Patrick didn't leave everything to me." Suddenly, I could see more problems in the marriage than I had first thought.

I wasn't surprised by her complaints about Patrick. I knew the statistics. The Institute for Women's Policy Research reported that women spend two hours more than men doing domestic chores each day. Every month, four or five of my female patients complained about their husband's blindness to the half-eaten food on the counter and the dirty socks piling up next to the bed. I always nodded, prepared for the angry words I knew would follow: *Can't he do anything on his own? I feel like my husband is another child.*

I thought about my patient Alison, an elementary school teacher, married to Mark, a landscaper. When they had their kids, she believed their work schedules would complement one another. She would assume primary responsibility for their sons during her summer vacation from school; her husband would do the same during the winter when the landscaping business slowed down. Unfortunately, the system hadn't worked as she had expected. She kept her end of the bargain, but Mark didn't keep his. When she got home from school in January and February, Mark would be napping on the couch, the kids would be glued to the television screen, and the dishes would be piled up in the sink.

Meghan's sigh interrupted my thoughts. "I wanted my marriage to be different from my parents," she said.

"In what way?" I asked.

Her parents had a traditional division of labor. Her dad was a successful businessman who worked long hours and did very well for himself, making enough money so his wife never had to get a job. She stayed home to take care of Meghan and her brother. Meghan had envisioned a different kind of marriage. "My career is important to me, just like Patrick's career is important to him. I thought we would be dividing the household chores more equitably," she said. "I didn't think I would be doing so much more childcare and general cleaning up than he did."

Alison, Meghan, and my other female patients had grown up in a society that paid lip service to the ideal of men and women sharing domestic responsibilities. Yet they ended up disappointed with their husbands who didn't shoulder their share of the parenting and household chores. No wonder they were unhappy.

———————

A car alarm in the parking lot outside blasted off and on, startling me. Meghan seemed not to hear it. "I don't know what to do," she finally said. "I always felt pretty much in control of my life. Now I feel so uncertain."

The version of Meghan I had been talking to until now was a self-assured mom who ran her family's domestic life and explained solutions to complicated calculus problems to her high school students. That version of Meghan was fading fast. When she had the rug pulled out from under her by her husband's change of heart about having a second child, her life no longer looked as she expected it to, and she was lost. I watched Meghan's face change.

She pursed her lips, looking like a little girl trying hard not to cry. Several faint lines of confusion on her forehead deepened. She blinked fast a few times.

"I feel so uncertain," she said again.

"I know," I said. "It takes courage to admit that."

I liked the new Meghan I was beginning to see. She seemed more vulnerable, willing to show me some cracks in her armor.

We were coming to the end of the session. Meghan paused. I could see she wanted me to point her in the right direction. I racked my brain for a way to sum up the therapy hour, but nothing came to me. "It's okay to let yourself be confused," I finally said.

She uncrossed her legs again, leaned forward, and frowned. "What do you mean?"

"It's okay not to know what to do."

"I don't like the feeling," she said.

"No one does. But accepting you won't have any answers for a while takes the pressure off."

I could have been talking to my younger self. That version of me assumed my life would unfold according to a well-thought-out plan. I had no idea how little I knew. Even if I had, I doubt I would have had the courage to acknowledge it.

Meghan scrunched up her forehead. She raised her eyebrows. "I guess so," she said.

Her skepticism was okay with me. Admitting her uncertainty was a big first step, and it would take a while for her to get used to the idea she didn't have all the answers. For a therapist, confusion was a good place to begin.

CHAPTER 4

LISA

"**M**y life feels empty without Greg," Lisa told me at the end of her first month of therapy. With school out for the summer, she didn't have her job as a teacher's aide to distract her from her misery. Two of her adult children still lived at home and spending time with them gave her something to think about other than her marriage. Nevertheless, their presence was a strain. She could hear them rummaging around the kitchen at night, looking for something to eat while she sobbed in bed. She didn't want them to know how upset she was.

Lisa had decided not to discuss Greg with her kids. No matter how angry she felt toward him, she didn't want to poison their relationship with him. He was still their dad, after all. I complimented her on her wise decision.

"I know it is the right thing," she said. "Sometimes, it's tough to bite my tongue. What I really want to do is tell them every single sordid detail about Greg's affair." She frowned, stared out the window, and looked back at me. "I still miss him. Even though I wish I didn't."

"It is the attachment," I said. "People remain attached to people they know aren't good for them. Think about the way the physically abused children you have worked with at school remain bonded to their parents."

Lisa shrugged. "Maybe Greg *is* good for me," she said. "I can't tell."

I smiled a little. "Sure, perhaps you're right. It is just something to keep in mind." I was pleased Lisa disagreed with me. It was a positive step for her to practice standing up for herself, even with me. She had asserted herself with Greg as well, refusing to let him move back home no matter how many times he asked. Therapeutic progress, I thought.

At the end of the summer, Lisa returned to teaching. She had been looking forward to it. Work was a life-saver, giving her something to think about besides Greg. Another female patient, forty-year-old Tanya, told me the same thing when she came to see me during her own crisis. "When I get dressed in professional clothes to go to work, I forget my husband is a lying cheater," she said. "When I get home, I can cry and scream all I want."

————

On a chilly afternoon in late September, I listened for the clunky metallic sound the heat made in my office when it switched on, but it was silent. I reminded myself to ask the landlord to turn on the heat and slipped on a bulky sweater I kept on my coat rack for days like this. Today would be Lisa's sixth session, and she showed up for her appointment early.

"I can turn on the space heater to warm the place up," I said, rubbing my hands together to get the circulation going. I looked out the window and glimpsed a few yellow leaves on the tree outside. Autumn could be a challenging time for many of my patients; they dreaded the short, dark days of New England's winter because their mood often worsened. My twenty-five-year-old patient, Katie, was one of these people. She had been diagnosed with depression when she was eighteen, and every winter since then had been hard on her. Her mood worsened. Her motivation dwindled. She felt like she had a lead weight on her shoulders. She slept fifteen hours a day and still felt tired when she dragged herself out of bed in the morning.

"Seasonal Affective Disorder is the official name for what people often call winter blues," I said. "Probably caused by the way in which decreased sunlight lowers the activity of the neurotransmitter serotonin."

I wondered how Lisa would fare once winter set in. She didn't have Katie's history of depression. Could the grief she felt about her marriage trigger an episode anyway?

My eyes traveled from the tree outside my window to her face. Lisa looked oblivious to the diminishing daylight. The chill in the air didn't seem to be affecting her mood either. She wore a bright pink cardigan over her blouse, a pencil skirt, and low heels. While she was always well dressed, she looked particularly fashionable today. Perhaps the return to her job as a teacher's aide had improved her outlook. I took a second look at her wide smile, feeling confused.

The session felt different from the previous ones. Lisa laughed a lot. Her speech seemed less pressured. Even the topics she discussed changed; we mostly chatted about her kids and her job. The shift in her tone reminded me of the more easy-going sessions that occur when a patient feels ready to wind down therapy. Yet this was only Lisa's sixth session. What was going on?

Despite my questions, I was enjoying the improvement in her mood. I even patted myself on the back for helping her so much. When we came to the end of the hour, I squinted at my clock to see the time. Then Lisa coughed.

"I'll make this my last appointment," she said.

My head jerked back towards her. "Your last appointment?" My voice squeaked out in surprise. "How come?"

"Greg and I have been talking on the phone every night," she said.

She flipped her hair back away from her eyes. It looked like she had just had it cut and streaked with even more blonde highlights. She smiled at me. I smiled back. A tug of uneasiness pulled on me. I shifted my weight to get my back comfortable against the hard surface of the chair.

"What do you two talk about?"

"The kids. The happy times our family had together."

She and Greg had gone out to dinner several times over the past two weeks and agreed they didn't like being apart. I watched the corners of her mouth flicker upward. Her brown eyes looked bright and sparkly. I nodded, uncertain about what to say next.

"You know," she said. "We miss each other. We thought we should spend more time together, eventually even live together again."

Suddenly, the right words came to me. *Don't let him move back into your house.* I could say it in a loud, firm voice. Of course, I didn't say anything at all. I struggled to make sure my lips didn't sink into a deep frown. I had made this mistake with a previous patient, Angela, and I wanted to avoid making it again.

Angela was a nurse, married for fifteen years, with two pre-teen daughters. I had treated her for eight months several years earlier. She came to see me because she was unhappy in her marriage. Each week she told me a different story about her husband, Harry. Harry spent little time with the family. Harry followed her around the house yelling at her in front of their children. Harry was even scrolling through a dating site. After two months of this, I hated Harry. A sharper tone edged into my voice each week when I asked her why she stayed married to him.

One day Angela didn't show up for her appointment. She didn't call me back when I phoned to find out if she had forgotten and wanted to rebook. I never heard from her again. Right away, I knew I had made a mistake. I hadn't respected her timing. I had been careless with my tone. I had failed to empathize with her desperate need to stay with a husband she could barely tolerate. My therapeutic mistake taught me a lesson as important as any I learned in my four years of graduate school: be gentle when challenging a patient's decision.

"I wonder if you are moving too quickly," I said to Lisa in my best, soft, whispery therapist voice. I wanted her to continue treatment so we could explore why she gave her husband so many chances.

"I don't think so," she said.

I took another look at her. Her outfit was so pretty, and her eye shadow seemed to have a sheen of glitter in it. The reason why her mood had lifted was becoming apparent: she believed she and Greg would have a future together. I wasn't entirely surprised by her decision. I only had to think back to Lisa's appearance when I first met her: wide eyes bordered by dark circles, sighs so deep and loud they bounced off the walls in my office, and nervous energy vibrating throughout her body. She had depended on Greg for the past thirty years and was terrified she would have to take care of herself. Lisa wanted her marriage to work more than she wanted anything else. Who was I to take issue with that? When my marriage unraveled, I felt just as she did right now.

Lisa buttoned her sweater. We sat there, smiling at one another. "What do you think?" she said.

"About what?"

"Me and Greg."

"I don't know," I said. "What I think is less important than what you think."

"I miss him. I think it is worth giving our marriage another try."

"You don't have to let him move back in," I said. "You can spend time together and live apart. Kind of test each other out. See how it goes. There is no rush." In my mind, I was flashing a bright yellow light at her.

Lisa was fumbling with her purse, not looking at me. My warning sign hadn't registered. I felt tempted to lay out all the reasons why her decision didn't make sense. I didn't want to say goodbye, and I was worried she was making a mistake. Then I remembered my heavy-handed approach with Angela and realized I should handle Lisa with care. "Are you sure you don't want another appointment?" I said.

"I'm sure."

"You can always come back."

She stood up and grabbed her purse.

"How about seeing a marriage counselor before you get back together? I can recommend someone."

"Yeah, maybe," she replied. "I don't think we will need to."

———

I locked my office door and went out to the car. The drive between my office and home took fifteen minutes. I used the time to decompress from the day, thinking about what to make for dinner and which TV show to watch.

I walked in the door and slid a frozen Trader Joe's chicken tikka masala into the microwave. Then I switched on *The Great British Baking Show* and sat on the sofa, spooning the food into my mouth. Those bakers making a fancy frosted cake weren't holding my attention; I was worried about Lisa. Sure, her relationship with Greg appeared to be growing closer. Nonetheless, her husband had promised fidelity and betrayed her so many times. If she gave him another chance—for the fifth time, I thought, although I had lost count by now—I was sure he would break her heart.

I shook my head back and forth, trying to clear it out. I felt concerned that the difficulties I had had with my husband influenced my view of Lisa and Greg. Perhaps Greg could change in ways Tom couldn't. Yet when I recalled Lisa's stories about her husband, more and more doubts popped into my mind. In all his telephone conversations, text messages, and emails, Greg had glossed over his "mistake" as he called his affair, without any concrete plan about how to avoid a similar mistake in the future. On top of this, I couldn't figure out why Greg kept trying to reconcile with Lisa. He had gone back to the woman he was having an affair with so many times, he must have a deep attachment to her.

Why was Lisa taking what looked to be an enormous risk? Psychotherapists often say past behavior predicts future behavior, and Greg's repeated instances of infidelity suggested a pattern he seemed unlikely to break. Although Lisa saw the pattern, she couldn't escape her fears of being on her own. Greg had always promised to take care of her. She had depended on him to manage her life. Lisa had gone right from her mother's home to the home she had made with Greg. She didn't have the confidence she could take care of herself. So, if there was even the slightest possibility the marriage might work out, Lisa was willing to take the chance.

––––––––––

I switched off the TV and wandered into the kitchen for a late-night snack of saltine crackers with sweet, sticky strawberry jam. Comfort food. This had become a common pattern on the nights when I was preoccupied with a patient, wondering if I had done enough to help her.

When I started practicing psychotherapy, I assumed self-doubt was normal for a new therapist. I thought over time, once I had more experience, all my patients would get better, and I would no longer worry if I had done a good job. But that hasn't been the case.

Sometimes I've thought about whether I would have more consistent success if I followed a particular type of psychotherapy. There are many schools of thought about the best approach to treatment. Psychodynamic therapists, for example, help patients understand how the family they grew up in shaped them. According to this theory, insight into family dynamics will lead to change. In contrast, cognitive/behavioral therapists encourage patients to recognize how their distorted thinking affects their mood. These therapists want their patients to identify their automatic, negative thoughts and replace them with more positive, rational ones.

Some research indicates cognitive/behavioral treatment, particularly for anxiety disorders, is the most successful form of psychotherapy. However, other studies, including one provocatively entitled "Are All Psychotherapies Created Equal?" in *Scientific American*, suggest that different treatment approaches are equally efficacious. Consequently, many therapists practice in an eclectic fashion, as I do, using whichever theory best addresses the patient's difficulty. I like to think my approach is flexible, tailored to the kind of problem the patient brings to me. Still, sometimes I imagine myself throwing spaghetti on the wall in my therapy office to see what sticks.

On one of those days when I was preoccupied with my self-doubt, I scrolled through various websites until I found an *Aeon* magazine research report by Helene Nissen-Lie. She found that therapists with varying experience levels all felt some self-doubt and suggested that self-doubt can even be a positive trait. The report encouraged psychotherapists to listen to their patients' feedback and to self-correct their approach, as I had done between my Angela debacle and meeting Lisa. However, there was one thing which these researchers neglected to consider: even if self-doubt was a good basis from which to hone one's professional skills, it didn't feel good.

It was late—time for bed. I pictured Greg giving up his girlfriend, coming home on time each night to make Lisa feel important to him, not a disposable piece of trash. Oops, where did the word "trash" come from? It was easy to remember. It was the feeling I had with Tom more than thirty years earlier.

CHAPTER 5

ELLEN

My college roommate, Patty, introduced me to Tom in the fall of our senior year. She was my closest friend and knew how much I wanted a boyfriend. Late at night in our apartment I would sprawl on her bed, telling her stories about my disappointing social life. In junior high school I had been the target of a group of mean girls, as they would be called decades later. Every day I walked past their lunch table in the school cafeteria in terror, waiting for them to smirk, giggle and point at me. I felt like the bearded lady in the circus.

By the time I got to high school the mean girls had moved on to other targets, and I made new friends with shy girls who were studious like me. One particular characteristic drew us together: we hadn't mastered the art of snaring a boyfriend. This was the kiss of death for a teenage girl in the mid-1960s; a girl's success was measured by the presence or absence of a boyfriend. Without one, we fell to the bottom of the social hierarchy, invisible to everyone except ourselves.

For dating advice, I turned to popular teen magazines, like *Seventeen.* Many of the articles were devoted to how to attract a boy. I read about the long, stick-straight, fashionable hairstyle of the day and the most flattering bathing suit style for my figure. I learned the feminine way to act, deferring to a boy and never challenging his opinion. Nonetheless, no matter how many hours I spent studying these articles, my romantic life did not improve. No one asked me to the Junior Prom. No one asked me to the Senior Prom. I was mortified. What was I doing wrong?

Patty shook her head and looked sympathetic. "Did you date anyone during your freshman and sophomore years of college?"

I had a boyfriend freshman year who broke up with me after three months. In my sophomore year, I stared at a cute guy on the other side of the college cafeteria for several weeks. Finally, he asked me out. Though after our one date, he never spoke to me again. I saw myself as someone who couldn't hold a boy's interest for very long, and I feared it was due to my own failing. Each day, as I walked to my classes, my eyes darted from one kissing couple to another. I worried I would never be like them and felt a growing sense of alarm. "Maybe it will never happen," I said to Patty.

My desperation for a boyfriend embarrassed me. This was 1972, the height of the women's liberation movement, and Patty and I identified as feminists. We no longer called each other girls, referring to ourselves as women instead. We purged ourselves of all the symbols of women's oppression: out went the blue eye shadow matching my eyes, the bright pink, plastic hair rollers that cut into my scalp, and, of course, my bra. In my women's history class, the teacher quoted a common feminist slogan of the time, "A woman without a man is like a fish without a bicycle." I knew

I was supposed to feel proud about being an independent, single young woman. Yet I wanted a boyfriend as much as when I was a young teenager, reading the dating advice articles in *Seventeen*.

————

Patty pointed Tom out to me one night in the library, where we had gone to study. "He's cute and in my history class," she whispered. He was sitting in a carrel with a large pile of books on the desk in front of him, scribbling on a long, yellow legal pad. When Patty stopped to talk to him about an upcoming exam, a smile lit up Tom's entire face. I was taken aback. Most boys I had met in college weren't very expressive, but he looked like someone who didn't hide his enthusiasm. He seemed so open and innocent. As the two of them talked, I heard Tom's soft-spoken voice. It sounded unpretentious and gentle, the voice of a boy with nothing to hide. He stood up when Patty and I got ready to leave the library. He was tall, with pale skin and long dark hair. He had a bushy, friendly-looking mustache.

"I'm leaving too," he told us.

We made our way out the front door, me on one side of Tom and Patty on the other. I smelled the woody odor of pipe tobacco clinging to his hair. Patty and Tom talked about their history class. They agreed the course was a bear, with 150 pages of reading every night. Still, Tom loved the class. The best course he had taken in college. There was his bright smile again. A good-looking boy who loved to learn.

Over the next few weeks, I made sure I "bumped" into Tom every evening in the library. We got to know each other when I pulled up a chair next to the carrel where he studied. Mainly, we discussed our classes. I was a psychology major and a history minor. He was interested in math. He seemed so different from other guys I met in college, who blabbed on about themselves. Tom asked me questions and appeared to want to get to know me. I knew I wanted to get to know him, too.

All fall, we hung out together at his apartment. He sat hunched over his books at his desk, smoking his pipe and concentrating on a paper he was writing. I propped myself up on the pillows on his bed to read. I began staying overnight at his apartment, and in the morning, he made his mother's scrambled egg recipe for me.

When winter came, we went ice skating on a nearby pond. The cold air turned Tom's pale skin pink, and I rubbed my wooly mittens against his face to warm him. We walked back to Tom's apartment late in the afternoon and made hot chocolate. The sweet smell of cocoa powder floated through the air. After he washed the dishes, he wrapped me in his arms and told me he loved me. I was twenty-one years old and had been waiting to hear those words from a boy my entire life.

———————

In the spring of my senior year, I discovered my grades weren't high enough to enroll in a clinical psychology program as I had hoped. I had no idea what I would do next. The comfortable cocoon of college was ending, and I was supposed to be ready to step into adulthood. But I didn't know where I wanted to live or what kind of job I was qualified for. Beginning adult life on my own felt like sailing around the ocean in a small dinghy.

When Tom suggested I live with him in New York City, where he would go to graduate school, I jumped at the chance. Decades later, I wished I could have grabbed this young woman by the shoulders and shaken her. "Don't be afraid," I would have said.

"You can leave college and go out in the world by yourself." I doubt I would have even listened to my own words of encouragement, however.

Tom and I moved into a six-floor walk-up in New York in September. Within the first month, I got off the subway, noticed the zipper on my purse was open and discovered someone had stolen my wallet. A few weeks later, a teenage boy and girl followed me into the apartment lobby. When I turned around to say hello, I saw the boy holding a shiny, sharp knife blade about six inches from my face. They didn't have to say a word. I knew exactly what to do. I took the money out of my wallet and handed it to them. As soon as they left, I flew up the six flights of steps, threw myself in my apartment, and bolted the door shut.

New York was beginning to feel like a mistake. I felt unsafe. I missed Patty. The only job I could get was as a bank teller, and I hated it. Then, one Sunday in October, after we had been living together for about a month, Tom and I had our first fight. We were eating breakfast, and I asked him if he wanted to go to the corner Chinese restaurant for dinner. He shook his head.

"Why not?" I asked.

"I'm busy," he said.

I lobbied hard. We wouldn't even need to get on the subway. It would be a quick meal. Tom could come back and finish the paper he was working on.

"No," he repeated.

"One hour," I said. "Then we'll be back home."

Tom remained quiet.

"Come on," I said, speaking in a louder voice than I had ever used.

Tom stood up in the middle of my sentence and turned his back on me. He walked out of the kitchen, crossed the living room, stepped into the bedroom, and slammed the door shut. I followed his path, grabbed the cold doorknob and opened it.

"What's wrong?" I asked.

He picked up a book to read. "Nothing," he said.

"I'm not finished talking," I said.

Tom flipped open the book and turned over several pages.

"Come on, talk to me."

His eyes remained glued to the page, and he refused to utter a word. I walked back into the kitchen to wait for him to come out, assuming we would soon make up. But he didn't budge. I felt sick to my stomach and panic-stricken. I breathed quietly to hear what he was doing in the bedroom.

Two hours later, I made dinner, pushed the food around the plate, and finally threw it out. The honking car horns on the street outside the apartment hurt my head. When I walked into the bedroom to get ready for bed, Tom got up, gathered his pajamas into his arms, and went to sleep on the couch.

I woke up before Tom the next morning and left for work. All day long I sat on my stool in the bank trying to concentrate on making customer deposits. I worried about what Tom's mood would be like when I got home. As soon as I opened the apartment door and walked into the kitchen, I saw him at the stove, with his back toward me.

"Hi," I said.

He didn't say anything at all. Instead, he placed a piece of roast chicken on my plate and his, and he sat down to eat without even looking up at me. I swallowed hard to get the smallest bite of food down my throat. The only noise in the room was the tinny sound of our forks scraping against the plates. After we ate, I cleared the table and washed the dishes. Tom retreated to the living room, and I heard the rustling sound of him turning the pages. While he slept on the couch for a second time, I tossed and turned in our bed all night. No one had ever given me the silent treatment for days before.

————

The following day, forty-eight hours after our fight began, Tom finally broke the ice.

"Goodbye," he said right before I left for work.

"Goodbye," I said.

When I came home from work, we said hello and made small talk throughout the evening. Do you want to go grocery shopping tomorrow? What about a trip to the laundromat? By the next day, the fight was over. As the months passed, however, I couldn't avoid arguments that led to the silent treatment. "What about a weekend visit to Boston," I said one Thursday afternoon. "We can stay in Patty's apartment."

"I'm too busy."

"Just one night?"

"Not interested."

I pushed some more. We were young; I wanted the two of us to enjoy ourselves. Wouldn't it make our relationship even better? Nothing worked. Every effort to bring us closer together seemed to backfire.

By now, I had given up *Seventeen* magazine and was reading *Ms.* magazine, and I understood, in theory, a woman's voice should be equal to a man's voice. Yet each time I argued with

Tom, he resorted to the silent treatment. It didn't matter whether I used my voice or not; he didn't want to listen to it. So, after a while, I stopped trying to talk to him.

There was so much I didn't understand back then. I didn't recognize Tom didn't share my need for companionship. I had never heard about a pursuer/distancer relationship: a dysfunctional dance where the pursuer strives to bring their partner closer to them, and each effort causes the distancer to retreat further away. I would observe many couples who interacted this way once I became a psychotherapist. However, my twenty-three-year-old self didn't see I was a pursuer and Tom the distancer. And, I didn't know the word "stonewalling" could be used to describe someone like my boyfriend, who refused to talk when he was angry. Nor was I aware that this behavior increased the likelihood of a couple splitting up.

The thought of losing Tom terrified me. I knew that much. *Try to understand your feelings*, my older therapist self would have told the younger version of me. At the time it didn't occur to me to try to figure out why I felt this fear.

Our lease was coming up for renewal in a couple of months. When I asked Tom what he thought about our future, he shrugged. "I'm not making any promises," he said.

Perhaps it would be good for us to live apart, I thought. It could just be temporary. So I decided to move to Boston, where Patty lived, and enroll in a graduate history program at Boston University. I would have liked to say I was focused on creating a new life. The truth was I hoped Tom might miss me and appreciate me again. At least he had once loved me. I didn't know if anyone else ever would.

CHAPTER 6

ELLEN

"**M**eet me under the Arc de Triomphe," Patty had written to me in February when I was still living in New York with Tom. Why not? Tom and I weren't getting along at that point, and he didn't seem to care what I did. I had saved enough money from my bank teller job to take a trip. I was thrilled to have a chance to go to France.

In July, I got off the plane at Orly airport, took a bus heading to the city center, and there was Patty right where she said she would be, under the Arc de Triomphe. Over the next few days, we sampled all the luscious food we could afford. Each morning we bought croissants, a thin line of chocolate running right through the middle, and took them to a nearby café for a cup of steaming café au lait. Lunch was a baguette with silky, soft Camembert cheese. We ate the sweetest strawberries I had ever tasted for dessert, sitting along the Seine. Between our meals we marveled at one art museum after another: the Jeu de Paume with its impressionist paintings, the Rodin Museum, the museum of the Middle Ages called the Cluny Museum. Late in the afternoon we lounged on a bench in the Luxembourg Gardens, watching little children play with their toy sailboats.

Despite being shy, I talked with people I met on the train, in the youth hostel where we slept, and in the cafes where we drank our morning coffee. Even though I had been a mediocre French student, I asked for directions and ordered meals in the language. And, as terrible as my sense of direction had always been, I learned how to read a map. I had never considered myself competent before. Yet here I was mastering one travel challenge after another. I felt as if I had stumbled upon a buried treasure deep inside me. The resourceful and capable woman I became when I traveled was my best self, I would realize years later.

After six weeks of traveling around France, I flew back to Boston in late August and rented an apartment for graduate school. My clothes and books were still in New York, and I took the Greyhound bus back there to pack. The heat and humidity of late summer in New York smacked me in the face as soon as I got off the bus at the Port Authority Terminal. By the time I got to our apartment, I was drenched with sweat. I was nervous, too. Tom and I hadn't spoken in six weeks. I kissed him on the cheek, noticing his beard felt scratchier than I had remembered. We talked for a while about my trip and his summer research project. It was as if we were acquaintances trying to be polite to one another. Then, as he sat at his desk, I walked into the bedroom, ready to pack.

I stood in front of the open closet, slid my blouses off the hangers, folded them, and stacked them in neat piles in my suitcase. The books came next: novels in one box, history books for graduate school in another. I had just opened the bureau drawer when Tom stood up and leaned against the door frame.

"How's it going?" he said.

"Fine."

I piled my books in the boxes. Every once in a while, I looked up at Tom. His eyes looked sad. His teeth bit down and made a crease in his lower lip. His cheeks softened. I realized he would miss me, and I could see he knew it, too.

"Do you want me to drive you to Boston?" he asked.

I pressed the cardboard box flaps into place. My heart somersaulted in my chest.

"Really?" I said, looking up. "Sure, I'll tell my father he doesn't need to come."

The two of us loaded the car the next day. Once on the highway, we listened to the radio and chatted comfortably. We pulled into my new street, unpacked the car, and carried the suitcases and boxes up the stairs to my apartment. As Tom took one of the heavier boxes out of my arms, I was reminded of the young man I had first met in college: long hair, big smile, gentle laugh.

My graduate history classes began the Monday after Labor Day. I loved my courses, but each was more difficult than the last, with hundreds of pages of required reading each week and several research papers due during the semester. No matter how much schoolwork I had though, I always made time to talk on the phone to Tom, who was living alone in an apartment in New York.

At first he called me once a week. By the end of September he called me each evening and visited me almost every weekend. We would study together in my bedroom, Tom at my desk, me lying on my bed. We took long walks from where I lived in Allston to Harvard Square, stopping at the Cafe Pamplona for a coffee before walking home again. I wasn't pursuing Tom, and he wasn't running away from me. Finally, he told me he loved me again.

In February, we discussed moving to the same city. We would enroll in PhD programs in Philadelphia, Tom in math, and me in European history. Of course, we would live together. In retrospect, it felt like we slid into this plan, as if it was preordained.

On the first warm day in May, when I still lived in Boston and Tom in New York, I took the bus to visit him. We met at our favorite Greek restaurant in Greenwich Village. Our table was close to the grill where a hunk of lamb rotated on a large skewer, filling the restaurant with a deep, meaty scent. Tom cleared his throat, just as I was about to put my souvlaki sandwich into my mouth. "Do you want to get married?" he asked.

I placed the sandwich down on the plate and looked up at him. We had never talked about marriage before. In the back of my mind, I assumed our move to Pennsylvania would be a test of our relationship to see if we would get along when we lived together again. Nevertheless, my heart fluttering in my chest told me I wanted Tom to make a commitment to me. What more of a commitment could I ask for than marriage? Had I been honest, I would have just answered "yes." Instead, I told Tom I wanted to think about it, believing a decision like marriage required serious, mature thought.

On the bus trip back to Boston, I weighed the pros and cons of getting married. On the one hand, I was wary of marriage, having read enough feminist literature to see how easy it was for a couple to fall into traditional roles of husband and wife. I didn't want that for myself. But Tom and I rarely argued over household chores. On the other hand, I believed the vows people took when they married strengthened their commitment to one another. Why wouldn't I marry him, I thought?

The following weekend I took the bus back to New York and met Tom at "our" Greek restaurant. I leaned over to kiss him and inhaled the sweet scent of his pipe tucked into his shirt pocket. I offered the widest smile I could.

"Okay," I said, "Let's get married."

"Oh, I knew you would decide to marry me all along," he said.

———

At first, everything about our wedding looked like it would fall into place. Two weeks after we told my parents we were getting married, Tom and I spent several evenings around their kitchen table nailing down wedding details. Nothing fancy, we all agreed: my parents' backyard, a justice of the peace, a caterer, and a band.

The next week I bought a wedding dress, ivory colored with Mexican embroidery on the bodice that made me feel like an untraditional bride. Two weeks later we purchased the rings. Then one warm evening, as we walked around my parents' neighborhood, I asked Tom where he wanted to go on our honeymoon.

"Nowhere. School starts the week after our wedding. We don't have time for a honeymoon. We don't have the money."

I stared at him, my mouth agape. I had always imagined a romantic trip would be one of the highlights of getting married. "Come on," I argued, "think of all the memories we will have when we are older." Tom just shook his head. He repeated his position: not enough time and not enough money.

"I really want to go on a honeymoon," I said.

"We can't," he said.

At this point another woman may have given up the idea. Maybe I just had to find a destination that would appeal to Tom. I went through the list. We could fly to California where his grandmother lived, and she might put us up for a few days. Or a quick, easy, fun trip to Montreal. My husband-to-be rejected both these ideas.

I had had such a fine time traveling with Patty; I wanted to have the same kind of experience with Tom. "What about camping in the Delaware Water Gap?" I finally asked. The last time I had been camping was in Girl Scout camp, twenty years earlier. I didn't like it back then, and I doubted I would like it now. Still, I was desperate and wanted some kind of trip to mark the occasion of our wedding, the start of our new life. A camping honeymoon was better than no honeymoon at all. Tom loved his summer camp. How could he say no to that? Yet he did.

Tom and I walked to the car and slid in. He gripped the steering wheel. I sagged against the seat as if I were a deflated balloon. Neither of us said anything. We were getting married in a few weeks and didn't want to fight. I considered various scenarios until I came up with one that would make everything okay. Maybe Tom was right: money and time were tight. We could take a trip in the future. We would have the rest of our lives to travel together. Besides, the importance of a honeymoon paled in comparison to how much I valued the love Tom expressed to me.

———

The night before our wedding, Tom's parents gave a rehearsal dinner for my family and his, along with several close friends. I had looked forward to it: plenty of food, champagne, and a band for dancing. The first hour went well. A waitress threaded her way through the guests, offering people pigs in the blanket stuck with toothpicks. Finally, we all sat down to a prime rib dinner.

Around 9 pm, the pianist laid his hand on the keys and played his first chord. My parents sprang up to dance. They had been dancing together throughout their thirty-two-year marriage and, as the band played, they glided across the dance floor with the grace of two professional figure skaters. I looked over at Tom's dad, Ernest. He was drunk and running around the dance floor like an out-of-control eight-year-old. I watched him careen left and right, nearly side-swiping my mom. Tom's mom, Doris, was nowhere to be seen.

I grabbed Patty by the arm and dragged her into the ladies' room.

She leaned against the sink. "What's wrong?"

I explained how Ernest's behavior made me cringe inside. He was acting like the kind of loud, drunk, obnoxious man I had always steered clear of. He's excited, she reminded me. His son is getting married tomorrow. Give the guy a break.

Perhaps I could have cut him some slack if I hadn't always felt uncomfortable with how he treated Tom's mom, his quiet and submissive wife. "Browbeaten" was the word my father would use to describe her a decade later. When Ernest spoke to his wife, he usually teased her in a way that made clear he didn't respect her opinions. Their marriage looked so different from the one I hoped Tom and I would have. Ernest and his wife led separate lives, rarely going anywhere together. Until now, I had assumed Tom wouldn't turn out like his father, and our marriage would look more like my parents' marriage than his. As I watched Tom's dad, I started to have my doubts.

"You can always get a divorce," Patty said.

We stood looking at one another a few seconds more. What was she talking about? I had thought carefully about my decision. These must be normal, pre-wedding jitters. Tom loved me, and, of course, I loved him.

I heard the squeak of the ladies' room door open and the click-clack of high heels walking towards us. I put my finger over my lips. I ran a comb through my hair and straightened the neckline of my dress. There was nothing left to say. In less than twenty-four hours, Tom and I would be husband and wife.

CHAPTER 7

MEGHAN

The early summer heat wasn't helping anyone's mood. I walked from my car into the office building, feeling like I was trudging through a steam room. The only consolation was that my overly air-conditioned office would provide refuge from the oppressive heat. I positioned my chair under the ceiling vent, opened my appointment book, and saw today would be Meghan's therapy session.

When I ushered her in, I noticed a fine sheen of sweat on her cheeks. Apart from that, she looked tidy in her khaki shorts and a loose t-shirt. She frowned and leaned against the back of the chair, covering the same territory in this second session as she had in the first. For twenty minutes she complained about Patrick. He still hadn't decided if he wanted a second child. He continued doing only the minimum around the house to help.

Meghan paused. She had reached a dead-end and looked uncertain about what to do. She frowned. I frowned back. Her sense of helplessness triggered a similar feeling in me. I wasn't surprised, aware of the research cited by Stacey Colino in the *U.S. News*

& World Report that showed a listener feels a speaker's emotions when she unconsciously copies the speaker's facial expression, as I knew I was doing. It was as if the feelings were contagious, spreading from one individual to another. Helplessness was not a constructive feeling for a therapist to "catch." I forced my mouth into a smile rather than a frown, cleared my head, and redirected the conversation.

"Can you give me some background about the two of you?" I said. "How did you meet?"

Meghan and Patrick were both runners in college who practiced outside the gym. They saw each other daily and chatted as they warmed up before the run. "It was my sophomore year. He seemed to like me a lot, and I guess I just started to like him back."

"Was he your first boyfriend?"

"No, I dated another guy freshman year. He was exciting but unpredictable, with a temper. One of those bipolar types. I broke up with him. If I had stayed with him, the relationship would have probably become physically abusive. Patrick was different. Being with him was so safe."

I thought about the contrast between the two young men Meghan had dated: a temperamental boyfriend who excited and frightened her; and reliable Patrick, steady as a rock. It occurred to me that perhaps Patrick had become boring to her in ways she couldn't have predicted when they first met. I had seen this pattern before. My patient Joanne had married Tim, thinking he would offer her the stability she never had growing up with an angry, alcoholic father. By the time she came to see me, she had been married for twenty years and no longer felt interested in anything Tim said.

"Patrick never pushed hard to get his way," Meghan said. "Plus, I knew he cared for me much more than I cared for him. At the time, I liked that."

"Why?"

"I didn't have to worry about him leaving me."

I was surprised. I had imagined the self-assured Meghan sitting in front of me would have been a confident teenager. Now it seemed like she had been much more vulnerable than I had assumed. She reminded me of myself in college, and I knew the two of us were far from alone; the results of Victoria Dickerson's study in *Family Process* demonstrated that many young women struggled with a lack of self-confidence.

Two female patients, both recent college graduates, came to mind. Alyssa, a third-grade teacher, had made several new friends when she started teaching. Every Friday, a large group would go out for drinks after school. Even though she had fun, she often replayed the conversations with these women in her head, searching for anything she might have said to offend one of them. Alyssa couldn't escape the fear her co-workers wouldn't want to be her friend any longer. Another patient, Maria, had been a straight-A student in college. She majored in computer science and worked as a software engineer at a small start-up. Her boss had praised her work. Still, Maria couldn't shake the feeling she wasn't doing a good job and might be fired.

What was it with young women and their lack of self-confidence? And, perhaps more importantly, was there a connection between a young woman's questions about herself and her choice of a romantic partner? Had Meghan's lack of confidence propelled her into a relationship with Patrick, as I had been propelled with Tom? In this version of the story, we both were scared, worried young women running into a relationship to bolster our sense of self and avoid facing the world alone.

––––––––––

Meghan and Patrick dated throughout college. "In our junior year, Patrick's parents got divorced. He seemed lost and unable to take care of his life. I got more and more involved with helping him out. At first, I just helped him study for tests. Then I started to clean his dorm room for him and do his laundry."

"Really? Clean his dorm room?" I bit my lip so a giggle didn't fly out of my mouth.

Meghan noticed. "I know. Can you believe it? I thought I was being a good girlfriend. When I hear myself say it now, I don't even feel like I am the same person I was back then."

Her eyes opened and shut a few times as if she was trying to conjure up her former self. "Maybe it was my mom. She always took care of everything around the house. I assumed that was what a woman was supposed to do." Meghan stopped speaking for a few seconds. I imagined her trying to understand how she went from being Patrick's "good girlfriend" to his "good wife." Perhaps she saw how her decision at age nineteen laid the foundation for a dissatisfying pattern in her marriage.

I had my own set of thoughts running through my mind. I was questioning whether norms about female domesticity still influenced women's behavior, despite fifty years of a feminist movement. Or was Meghan an outlier, following the more traditional trajectory of her mother?

———————

The heat wave broke in August, and Meghan turned up in black slacks, ballet flats, and a long-sleeve blouse. It was two weeks before the start of school, and she had spent the previous day drawing up her lesson plans for the upcoming school year.

"What brought you into teaching in the first place?" I asked.

She always knew she wanted to be a teacher. It was similar to her plan of being a mom. She enjoyed working with children, and she wanted kids—the ones she had and the ones she taught—to be central to her life. "I also knew I wanted to be a math teacher," she said. "I really enjoy the logic of solving a math problem. That's when I am at my best."

Of course, I thought. Math was the perfect subject for a woman like Meghan who needed clear-cut answers to any problem; if only her life could resemble an algebra equation.

She was ready to look for a teaching job as soon as she graduated from college with her bachelor's degree in education. "Patrick graduated before I did and moved back to Boston, where we were from. I drove back and forth from my college in Vermont to visit him for a year. When I graduated, I wasn't sure what to do. I could move anywhere in the country and get a teaching job. It was exciting to think about."

This was one of the few times Meghan used the word "excitement" to describe any part of her life. I pictured a different version of her, not a buttoned-down teacher standing in front of her class. This one might be driving down the coast road in California with the convertible top down and the wind blowing in her hair.

"I also knew Patrick expected me to move to Boston to be near him." Meghan paused before she finished her thought. "So, I did." She pressed her lips together. Her shoulders sagged, and she leaned against the back of the chair.

Patrick proposed after they graduated, and she said "yes." A year into the marriage, Meghan wanted to buy a house. Patrick didn't have the time to come along, so she went house hunting alone. "I have always been interested in flipping houses," Meghan said. "My dad likes dabbling in real estate, too."

"Tell me more about your dad," I said.

"He is a very successful businessman. He bought a house for the family in one of the richer Boston suburbs. He's a pretty logical guy, and I take after him."

I was beginning to understand her better. She shared the characteristics of both of her parents. Like her mom, she bought into the traditional image of a woman's adult life without any questions, the version where the princess married the prince and lived happily ever after. Yet, in her determination to get a job done, Meghan was more like her father, a hard-hitting businessman. These two aspects of her personality felt like jagged puzzle pieces that didn't smoothly click into place, and I wondered how they would play out over time.

Meghan found a house she wanted to buy, and Patrick liked it, too. Once they moved into their new home, they decided to have a baby. Meghan had worked everything out with her pregnancy. She timed it so she gave birth to her daughter at the end of the school year, had the summer off with the infant, and went back to teaching in the fall. She hoped to do the same for her second baby, who she wanted to be just two years younger than her toddler.

"It was as if I was checking off the boxes," Meghan said. "Patrick loved me. Check. He wanted a family, just like I did. Check. He had majored in business in college and looked like he had a good career ahead of him. Check, check."

Meghan was even more of a planner than I had realized.

———

Psychotherapists conceptualize differences in patients in a variety of ways. The most common categorization system is by diagnosis, with the fifth edition of the *Diagnostic and Statistical Manual of Mental Disorders (DSM)* as the current guide. Therapists use these categories to make treatment decisions; the diagnosis of panic disorder, for example, might respond well to cognitive/behavioral therapy, the type of psychotherapy that encourages patients to replace their exaggerated, frightening beliefs, called thinking errors, with more logical ideas. The thought "I will die in a car accident in this fast-moving highway traffic" becomes "I have a good driving record, and the chance of a crash is small."

As helpful as the *DSM* can be, I have devised my own idiosyncratic categorization system. I divide people into two groups: those who try too hard to control their lives, "over planners," and those who don't try hard enough. Meghan fell into the first group. A patient I was currently seeing, Sarah, fell into the second.

Sarah was in her mid-twenties, with a seven-year-old boy, five-year-old twin girls, and an alcoholic husband. Every week she told me she couldn't leave the marriage; she didn't have any job skills, having married right out of high school and gotten pregnant immediately.

"What kind of job would you want if you could get one?" I asked.

She had trained as a hairdresser but had failed the licensing exam several times.

"Why don't you try again?"

"I won't pass," she said. "I only got through high school because I got extra time to finish my exams."

"How did that happen?"

"Once I was identified as having a reading disorder, I was given special accommodations for tests."

"Can you get more time for the hairdressing exam?"

Sarah shrugged. She was going to simply give up. I couldn't fault her; she had experienced failure so many times. Nevertheless, I saw the exam as her chance to turn her life around. I said to her what I often say to patients, struggling to find a way to direct their lives: "There are many parts of life you can't do much about. So you might as well *try* to take charge of the few parts of your life that you might actually be able to exert some control over." A week later, she asked me to write a letter documenting her disability, and the board of examiners gave her the extra time she needed to complete the exam, which she passed.

Meghan was an over-planner, thinking out every step to control her life. Over-planners are successful at achieving their life goals, according to research by Sarah Lindstrom Johnson and her colleagues. Yet Johnson found that expert planners faced their own set of challenges. They overestimated the power of their plans to shape their future and had trouble shifting gears when life went sideways, as Meghan's life appeared to be doing.

———

At the end of the session, she said, "I regret getting married when I was so young, only twenty-four. I didn't know enough about what I wanted in life to make a smart decision."

"Almost everyone regrets a decision they made in their early twenties," I said. "You're in good company." Of course, I was also thinking of my decision to marry at twenty-four. Lisa had married even younger than that. People who marry in their early twenties are more likely to divorce than people who wait until their late twenties or early thirties, according to the Institute for Family Studies. "If we could only turn the clock back, lots of people would make very different decisions from the ones they made when they were young," I said.

Meghan looked out the window. I suspected she was still trying to unpack why she had married Patrick in the first place. "I wonder if I was too preoccupied with what I thought I should do," she said. "Not what I wanted to do."

I heard a questioning tone in her voice I hadn't heard before, a new self-reflection. Then in a whisper, Meghan said when she got married, she hadn't thought much about what she felt for Patrick.

"Why not?" I asked.

She paused, looked down at the floor, and then up at me. Rather than answering my question, she launched into a story. "This isn't the first time I have seen a therapist to talk about Patrick," Meghan said. Her voice had the hushed quality of someone about to reveal an important secret. "I went the first time because I was interested in another guy, a teacher at school." A pale, pink blush was spreading over her cheeks. "It was early in my marriage. Mostly, all the teachers went out together after school on Friday. So, it was in a group. Still this guy and I would always sit next to each other at the end of the table. We had so much to discuss: our students, professional goals, and educational philosophy. I started to have feelings for him, and I could tell he was interested in me."

"What did Patrick think?"

"When I would come home to Patrick, he would ask me what this guy and I talked about. Just school stuff, I said. I wanted to change the subject because I didn't want Patrick to realize I was developing a crush on another man."

She spent several weeks with her first therapist trying to figure out what she should do. She weighed the pros and cons of her marriage. Should she give up her husband for a fling that might never go anywhere? It would be crazy, irresponsible, and immature. "You know," she said, "Millennials use the term 'adulting' to describe what it is like to grow up."

"What do you do when you 'adult'?"

"You leave adolescence behind and learn to do all the tasks adults need to do: pay your bills, get up to go to work on time, buy car insurance. Ending your marriage for a man who is practically a stranger is not what an adult does."

I hoped Meghan could see that adult dilemmas were more complicated than paying bills on time. I suspected we would return to this topic, and I knew I would explain my ideas about "adulting." This view had less to do with accomplishing tasks and more to do with deeper changes that can occur as people age: an ability to accept the errors we make in life decisions, a willingness to embrace uncertainty, and the courage to acknowledge we have less control in life than we ever imagined.

I glanced at Meghan's face. There were her feelings of confusion again. We both looked at the clock at the same time. The appointment was almost over. I had one more question to ask. "When you look back, why do you think you were interested in this other man?"

She took a moment. "Maybe my heart was telling me there was a problem with Patrick, and I didn't realize I should listen to it."

CHAPTER 8

LISA

Afrter I wrote a note about Meghan's progress in her chart, I gravitated to the comfy chair to check my voicemail and return a few phone calls. Sarah, the non-planner, had phoned to apologize for forgetting her session. I scribbled down her phone number, reminding myself to delay calling her back until my irritation about the forgotten appointment disappeared. The second message was from a new patient named Ruth, who wanted help with her panic attacks, one of my areas of specialization. I would return her call before I left for the day. The final voicemail was the biggest surprise. It was from Lisa, who I hadn't heard from in six weeks, requesting another appointment. Her abrupt decision to end therapy and reconcile with her husband had seemed rash to me, and I was pleased she had called.

In graduate school, I learned about how to approach the end of psychotherapy—called termination: review the patient's progress, discuss how she can handle problems in the future, and talk about the feelings evoked by saying goodbye to one another. With the process completed, the patient, now healed, was supposed to make a clean break from treatment. The therapist would remain behind, a closed chapter in a patient's life, knowing they had prepared her for independence.

I discovered many times through the years that my therapy practice never seemed to follow the model I learned about in school. My patients kept coming back. They would call me months or even years after their "last" therapy session to book another appointment. At first, I questioned if I had done an effective job with them. No one ever complained about that, however. Instead, they told me I already "knew their story," and they didn't want to start over with someone new. It made perfect sense to me; the year I met Lisa I had been seeing my therapist, Joe, off and on for over thirty years.

I no longer think of the last therapy session necessarily as a termination. It is a hiatus. And, I like telling people, "you can always return," as I had said to Lisa, knowing they can think of me if they need help again.

———

Several days later I ushered Lisa into my office. She was dressed in tailored black slacks and a purple print blouse. Her eyes had dark circles around them, just as they did the first time she told me about her husband's affair. Her face looked tired and drawn.

"What brings you back?" I asked.

"Greg isn't coming back home," she said softly.

"How come?"

She pushed her hair out of her eyes, looked down at her black pumps and sighed. She picked up her story where she had left off, six weeks earlier. While Greg continued living in the hotel, they decided to spend more time together. He took her out to dinner at a fancy restaurant several nights in a row. As they ate their meal, they discussed their kids. The older one had found a new job and the younger one was considering transferring to a different college. Those nights felt like old times. They were a couple again, the way they were before Greg had his affair.

Lisa paused. I shuffled through my mind, trying to find the best words to describe the situation. Greg was courting Lisa all over again. That was it. The months he spent begging her to come back to him hadn't worked. Perhaps a softly lit restaurant would lure her in. I tried to picture the scene. She and Greg might be sitting at a small table at Davio's, a popular, upscale Italian restaurant. A flickering candle on top of a starched, white tablecloth, gave the room a romantic glow. Light bounced off the dark, ruby-colored wine in their glasses. I imagined Greg reaching across the table and stroking Lisa's hand.

"What did those dinners feel like?" I asked.

"Sort of fun," she said.

"Sort of?"

Part of her enjoyed being wined and dined, and I understood how flattered she must have been by his attention. After all, she had felt rejected for many months because he was sleeping with another woman.

"What about the other part of you?" I asked.

"I knew we weren't talking about what I wanted to talk about."

"What was that?"

Lisa's face changed. Those wide, sad eyes narrowed. Her jaw locked into place. She looked angry now, not sad. "Greg's affair," she said.

Wow, I thought, we were getting somewhere. Until now, she had been so focused on holding on to Greg she hadn't considered what she wanted from him: a full accounting of his behavior. Finally, she seemed to be moving several steps closer toward being able to stand up for herself.

"What did you want to discuss about the affair?" I asked, although I could guess.

"I didn't think Greg understood what it did to me," she said. "The pain I felt when I discovered it destroyed me. It was a sense of loss as bad as if he had died. Worse. Because he caused me this pain through the choices he had made."

"It must have been like someone stabbed you with a sharp knife," I said, as the night Tom told me he didn't want children crept back into my mind.

Lisa nodded and took a deep breath. Then, in the safety of my office, her questions about the details of Greg's affair flooded out of her, like a dam breaking. How often did he sleep with this other woman? Where did they do it? Why did he get involved with her in the first place? What did this woman offer him he wasn't getting from Lisa? And, most importantly, since he worked with this woman, how would he prevent himself from continuing the affair?

These questions kept Lisa up at night. They went through her mind when she was cooking, working with a student at school, trying to concentrate on her daughter's story. She could never escape them. They made her feel like she was going crazy.

"Those questions are completely normal," I said. "Everyone whose partner has betrayed them becomes consumed by the details of the affair."

A flicker of surprise crossed Lisa's face.

"No, you're not crazy," I said.

I pictured another couple, my patients John and Ann, who also struggled with the aftermath of infidelity. John had been the unfaithful partner, and Ann discovered it in a particularly painful way. During a routine medical appointment, her doctor questioned her about the possibility of multiple sex partners. "No way," she replied and laughed as she told the story to John when he got home. He was quiet. "No way, right?" she repeated. John confessed he had slept with a woman he met at a work conference. Ann felt her entire life collapse. Like Lisa, she told me the questions about her husband's affair took over her mind so she could think of little else. "Obsession" was the word she used.

According to one expert on infidelity, Shirley Glass, the obsessive questions Lisa and Ann went through are typical of how people react to the trauma of discovering a partner's cheating. A man or woman whose spouse has been unfaithful feels as if their partner has violently assaulted them. While the marriage seemed safe before, now it appears threatening: the betrayed spouse feels as if they are living with a stranger who walks around with a knife tucked under their arm. Desperate to understand what has happened to them, these people become obsessed with finding out about the affair's details, just as Lisa was doing.

"So, what did you do?" I said.

One night Lisa decided to ask Greg her questions. She felt sick and scared about how he would react when she brought up his affair. In the past, Lisa, who hated confrontation, had always tried to avoid a fight with him. Yet she knew she had to say something.

"I said to him we have to talk about your affair."

I imagined the tension in the car that night: Lisa looking out the side window to avoid Greg's stare and his hands gripping the steering wheel. I had seen enough couples struggling with the aftermath of infidelity to know what it was like. The partner who had the affair felt ashamed and embarrassed about their behavior. Talking about it was the last thing they wanted to do because it meant facing the pain they had caused their spouse.

"He told me there was nothing to talk about. He had already admitted he made a mistake. The affair was over."

I glanced at Lisa and saw her sagging back into the chair, as if the disappointment in her husband weighed her down. She reached over for a tissue and blew her nose.

"Was that the end of it?"

Suddenly, she straightened up and leaned forward. "No." The word came out of her mouth like a loud hiss. She brought the same issue up on the phone the next day. "Of course, I was nervous." She wanted Greg to understand how much she needed to have her questions answered, but her husband wouldn't budge.

"I already told you, Lisa," he said. "I don't have anything more to say. It's over."

Maybe it was over for him, but it wasn't over for her.

Lisa explained Greg's refusal to discuss his affair made her feel even worse. She was in pain, and he wouldn't do the one thing that would help her.

"Come on, Lisa. It's time to move on," he finally said to her.

My heart sank. Greg was doing exactly the opposite of what Glass recommended the cheating partner should do. As Glass explained, the betrayer needs to act as the healer in the relationship by listening to their partner's questions—many of them repeated over and over—and answering them honestly. Of course, this is a difficult position for the betrayer to be in. It means acknowledging they had made a choice that hurt their spouse. Again, John and Ann came into my mind. Unlike Greg, John answered all of his wife's questions without being resentful or defensive. "It was hard and embarrassing," he said. "I understood Ann needed me to do this to help her get over my affair. Otherwise, the marriage didn't stand a chance."

I repeated Greg's words "move on" to myself, and a familiar feeling of frustration overtook me. I remembered the many times I had heard an unfaithful partner say the identical thing to their spouse. While "moving on" has a nice, upbeat ring to it, the phrase doesn't capture the complicated processes of dealing with your partner's affair. Shirley Glass suggested the pain is too acute and raw for anyone to be able to "move on." It was a trauma, and trauma takes a long time to heal.

Lisa had spent her married life deferring to Greg. At this moment, she was trying to stand up for herself. I wondered if she would give in to him or hold on to her own point of view. "What did you do next?" I asked.

She tried asking Greg the same questions a few more times: after work at a bar one night when they went out for a drink, standing outside their house when he came over to pick up his mail. He became increasingly irritated every time she brought up the topic. Finally, after they had gone over the same territory many times, Lisa decided I had been right. They needed marriage counseling, so she booked an appointment with a therapist who came highly recommended by a friend.

"How did it go?" I asked.

Lisa frowned and went on to describe the sessions. They had sat on the couch together, but Greg fidgeted a lot. She spoke first, telling the story of Greg's affair and their multiple separations. Before they could get back together, she needed to understand why her husband made his hurtful choice. The therapist asked Greg what he thought about Lisa's questions. "I told her the affair was a mistake. It's over." The therapist encouraged him to say more about his affair, but Greg repeated he had nothing to add.

The couple had several more appointments with the marriage counselor. Lisa was feeling increasingly hopeless about getting the information she needed from her husband to rebuild the marriage. Finally, the counselor tried a different approach. "What is one thing Greg could do that would mean something to you?" he asked Lisa.

She wanted him to get a new job. The woman with whom he had the affair still worked at his current company, and Lisa felt it was just a matter of time until the two of them started up again.

"What do you think, Greg?" the therapist said.

At first, Greg fought back. He didn't intend to continue his affair and didn't know why he should leave his company. But Greg's promises weren't enough for Lisa; he had broken them too many times. He needed to take the step she was asking of him. I studied Lisa as she was telling me this story. Her voice grew louder and firmer. I imagined her talking to Greg in her new tone, and I wondered if he was surprised to hear her talk this way. Finally, he agreed to look for a new job.

Over the following week, they spoke on the phone every night. Greg told her about another company where the boss seemed interested in him. The interview went well. He believed they were going to offer him a job. There was a hitch, though. The salary was a lot less than what he was making now.

"Don't worry about the money," Lisa told him. "We can live on less, if we need to."

A few nights later, Lisa detected a change in Greg. He stopped telling her about the opportunities at this new firm. He reminded her of their dreams of traveling together when he retired and the amount of money they would be giving up if he left his company.

I guessed where this conversation was headed. Greg didn't want to do what Lisa asked him to do. Would she go along with his ploy to get her to stop pressuring him to change jobs? When the two of them went into their next therapy session, Greg announced he had turned down the offer. "It will be better for both of us if I stay at my current job," he said. "We'll have so much more financial freedom when I retire."

Lisa was stunned. "I always knew money, fancy restaurants, and expensive hotels meant more to Greg than they did to me," she told me. She couldn't believe he would put money before her. Lisa never knew whether it was the money or the other woman. Perhaps he never really intended to end his affair.

"Then what happened?" I asked.

"I canceled the next appointment with the marriage counselor because I couldn't see any point in continuing," she said.

"What are you thinking of doing now?" I said.

"I have a feeling deep in my gut. This separation is going to be permanent. That's why I made another appointment with you. I have to decide if I should divorce Greg." Her voice trembled; her face looked pale. It was like she stood on a fault line in the ground, watching tall buildings sway back and forth.

"It's a big decision. You don't need to be in a rush to make it. We'll just pick up here again next week," I said.

CHAPTER 9

ELLEN

O n a cool Friday morning in April, Tom and I stood on the front porch of the marriage counselor's office. We avoided one another's gaze, as if we were strangers on a crowded bus. He grimaced, checked his watch, and tried to turn the unyielding doorknob several times. Finally, he rapped his knuckles hard on the door.

That morning I had woken up with a nervous, jangly feeling in the pit of my stomach. It had gripped me at breakfast as I tried to swallow a bite of toast and gulp down a few sips of bitter coffee. I didn't know what to expect from this appointment. All I had was Sally's positive experience with marriage counseling to go on.

Over the previous week, I had concocted a fantasy of the perfect outcome of our counseling session: Tom would change his mind and decide to have a baby with me. Deep inside, I understood marriage counseling would not offer a simple, easy cure, and I had tried to picture Tom in the counselor's office. Would his mouth open into a wide yawn, as it did when I tried to talk to him? And what about his jokes that had begun to look like a way to deflect a serious conversation? Would they pepper his answers to the counselor's questions as they did to mine? Some men might be comfortable with psychotherapy, but I doubted Tom would be one of them. Sports and politics were the subjects he liked to discuss, not feelings.

A few minutes later, Joe, our marriage counselor, bounded up the steps and shook our hands. He was a tall, thin man with blonde hair, a few years older than Tom and me. I guessed thirty-six or thirty-seven. He apologized for being late; he had just finished his daily run.

"Let's go into my office," he said.

The room was large and airy. A dollhouse and a large box of blocks stood in one corner and a desk piled high with books stood in the other. Sunlight streamed in through two large windows. I sat on a beige sofa and crossed my legs. Tom took the loveseat on the far side of the room. Joe settled himself on a comfortable-looking blue chair. He positioned the chair to be equidistant between Tom and me, as if he were a referee between two sparring boxers. More than thirty years later, I would flash on the position of this chair when I was counseling a couple who referred to me as the neutral country of Switzerland.

"What can I help you with?" Joe asked.

A long silence followed. The loud tick-tock of the tall, wooden grandfather clock sounded in the background. I squirmed in my seat. Finally, unable to stand one second more of silence, I said, "My husband has changed his mind about wanting kids." I waited for Tom to speak, but he just nodded at Joe. Another long silence. Joe looked at me, and I looked back at him. Tom's eyes darted back and forth, as if expecting someone to pounce on him. When

I began to provide marriage counseling myself, I would understand this expression. Men often came in with their female partners, fearing the counselor and their wife would gang up on them.

I glanced at Joe again, hoping for a clue about what to do. There was so much on my mind I wanted to say. First, we needed to discuss our dilemma about having children. In the previous two weeks, I had thought about our marriage a lot, and our conflict about a baby looked like the tip of the iceberg. Many deeper problems lay beneath. Tom and I didn't know how to communicate with each other. We avoided talking about topics that might lead to a conflict. Our current way of arguing—him ignoring me for several days and me pleading with him to tell me what was wrong—had gotten us nowhere. The script I had been following—appreciating Tom, pretending he hadn't hurt my feelings, accepting no relationship was perfect—hadn't resulted in a good marriage, after all. I hoped this appointment with Joe would be the new beginning the two of us needed.

———

Tom remained quiet. I was beginning to worry. Where would we go from here? Joe leaned back in his chair, stretched his long legs out in front of him, and waited. He had been practicing for ten years, and his easy-going manner made me realize he was undaunted by Tom's silence.

"I'd like to know more about your parents before we discuss the child issue," Joe said. "Sometimes peoples' expectations about what it will be like to have their own kids are shaped by their early family experiences."

I glanced at Tom who was looking at the ground. He said nothing at all, so I started talking about my family. My parents met in college and had been married for forty years. My dad was a patent attorney, my mom a high school science teacher. Their marriage wasn't perfect; my dad's new hobby, oil painting, frustrated my mom because he often preferred to stay home to paint rather than go out with her. Nonetheless, their shared interests of science, traveling, and opera drew them together. I admired the companionship of their marriage.

"What about you, Tom?" Joe asked.

Tom said his father worked as a businessman. His mother stayed home, raising him and his older brother.

"What was their marriage like?" Joe asked.

I clamped my mouth down tight, so I wouldn't interrupt. I knew what I would say if Joe had directed the question to me. Tom's dad worshiped hard work. On the surface, he always smiled at everyone, yet he never appeared comfortable in social situations. Tom's mom hadn't gone to college and spent her time doing housework. She was timid, never learned to drive, and relied on her husband to take her wherever she needed to go. Tom's parents looked like two people with little in common, living separate lives.

After a slight pause, Tom answered Joe's question. His dad was a strict man who got Tom and his brother up at 7 am on Saturday mornings so they would get their chores done. Then the family got in the car and drove to the hardware store. In the spring and summer, his father bought manure for his garden that he loaded into the back of the family station wagon. "The whole car smelled like shit," Tom said.

"Shit?" Joe said.

"Yes," Tom said, "I hated it."

"Do you think having a dad like yours affected how you might see yourself as a father?" Joe asked.

"I don't want to be anything like my own father," Tom replied, his tone sharp and tense.

"Why not?" Joe asked.

"He was too strict with us," Tom said. "I didn't like how he treated my mom. He wouldn't talk to her for days when she did something to make him mad."

I thought about the many arguments Tom and I had that ended up with him ignoring me. I could see his dad's way of getting angry resembled Tom's silent treatment. Would my husband recognize it, too? I was praying he did; it would be a turning point in our marriage.

"Are you afraid you'll end up like him?" Joe asked.

I considered pointing out Tom was already much like his father, but I remained quiet. I sat there, wondering what he was going to say. I wished he would admit that no matter how many qualities of his dad he disliked, he never stopped yearning for his father's approval. And it never came, not when we married nor when Tom completed his doctoral degree. It was a fool's errand, from my point of view.

Tom remained quiet. I saw him staring at the floor, shaking his head back and forth. His legs jiggled up and down, and I pictured a rocket right before take-off. Then, just when I expected him to talk about his fears about fatherhood, he launched into a diatribe about me. "It's my wife who is the problem. She's selfish. She's careless. I always need to be the heavy in the marriage, the grown-up."

My head jerked back and forth between my husband and the marriage counselor. What just happened?

At this point, my husband took over the session. He described more of my faults, and his voice grew harsher and rougher the longer he spoke. I didn't leave him alone on weekends to write the articles he would need to get tenure. I didn't understand how much pressure he was under to do well in his career. I wanted to travel, even though we didn't have enough money.

The hope I had been holding on to vanished. It was as if Tom had punched me in the gut, knocking the air out of me. I was confused and scared. I thought we would discuss the issue of having kids with the counselor. Yet Tom only talked about my failings. My mind replayed his accusations that I had been self-ish and careless. As I listened to him describe his unhappiness, I pulled my sweater tight around me, feeling as if a cold wind had whipped through Joe's office. Then it dawned on me. Perhaps the baby issue had been a red herring all along. The real problem was Tom didn't want me.

When he took a breath, I tried to defend myself. "I just wanted us to enjoy ourselves while we were still young," I said in an embarrassing, high-pitched, squeaky voice. "I thought it would be fun to do things together. Like my parents did." I looked at Tom, hoping to see him paying attention to my words. Instead, he was leaning against the back of his chair with his eyes trained on the ceiling, arms crossed over his chest.

In the remainder of the session, Tom voiced complaint after complaint about me. I pleaded with him, hoping to convince him I could do better. I wouldn't bother him anymore about going out together on weekends. I would never mention the word travel ever again. Now I finally understood him, couldn't we start to iron out our problems?

Joe checked his watch. "I know it's a bad place to stop. Marriage counseling can be hard work. It takes a while to sort things out." He stuck his hand in his jacket pocket, pulled out a pen, and began to fill out an appointment card.

"I'm not coming back," Tom said.

My heart sank.

"Don't you want to give counseling more of a chance?" Joe asked.

Tom just shook his head. "No."

Joe turned to me with a questioning look.

"Come on, Tom," I said. "Let's just try again."

He stood up and walked out the door.

"Here's the appointment card," Joe said. "Why don't you come back by yourself?"

I grabbed the card and ran to catch up with Tom. I tumbled into the passenger's seat, my fingers felt cold and clammy. "Why not make another appointment?" I said. "I *really* didn't know you were miserable."

"I'm not going back," he repeated as he turned the key in the ignition. The car growled to life. His hands tightened around the steering wheel. But he didn't say anything else at all.

For the next few days, Tom avoided me; as soon as I walked into a room he walked out. A few times I smiled at him, hoping he would smile back. Each time he looked away, not at me. Tom left for his teaching job in Maine on the third morning of the silent treatment, and I immediately called Sally. I replayed the session to her line by line. Had I done all those things Tom accused me of? Was I so terrible? For all my fears and fantasies about marriage counseling, I had never once imagined we would only attend one disastrous session. Nor did I suspect Tom was as angry at me as he turned out to be.

The next few days crawled by, and I was afraid of the mood Tom would be in when he returned. On Thursday afternoon, before he got home, I was rummaging around the file cabinet where we kept our checkbooks. Inside an ivory manila folder, I saw a letter in Tom's handwriting scrawled on a page of a yellow legal pad, addressed to our bank. I pulled the chair away from the desk and sat down to read it. *Please take my wife off my credit card account. I am getting a divorce.*

I sank down on the rocking chair, trying to figure out what to do. Was Tom going to tell me in person he was divorcing me or leave a note behind, pack up his things, and tiptoe out the door? I lay down on the bed, gripping the letter in my hand. Forty-five minutes later, my husband's heavy footsteps clomped up the stairs. He walked into our bedroom and turned on the light. I rolled over to face him.

"What's this letter about?" I asked.

"There is nothing more to say," he said. "I'm leaving. My brother is coming with a U-Haul truck to help me move my stuff out."

I was about to plead with him again, just as I did in the therapist's office. Give me another chance. I'll be better than I was. I didn't know you were unhappy. I opened my mouth to speak. Then I took another look at Tom's face. He didn't even look angry now. Just bored. Finally I understood this man would leave me, no matter what I said, and I decided I would never again ask him to give me another chance. When I looked back at the day, that was the only decision I was proud of.

After Tom left the bedroom, I opened the bureau drawer and took out my nightgown, a clean t-shirt, and my jeans. I shoved everything into my backpack. Then I trudged down the stairs to my car, trying to keep myself from drowning in the panic lurking in the periphery of my consciousness. I wasn't sure where to go, but I couldn't live in my apartment with Tom any longer.

For the next two weeks, I was a nomad. I bounced from the bed in Patty's study to the spare room of a colleague, Alexandra, another professor at Boston College. She was a woman I barely knew who offered me a place to stay when she found me crying in my office. Over dinner and two large glasses of white wine, Alexandra shared her view of how relationships end. "The dumper," she said, "needs to make the dumpee out to be the bad guy. Otherwise, they would have no reason for hurting someone they were supposed to love." I felt like Alexandra had handed me a small gem of a thought I hadn't considered before: Tom's accusations about me, whether or not they were true, provided him with the justification he needed to leave.

Her words stuck with me for decades. Once I became a therapist, I would repeat them to many patients struggling with the accusations their partners made as they were leaving. Later I realized how much the advice people gave me during this time in my life informed many of my therapy interventions, perhaps even more than the theories I studied in graduate school.

At the end of the week, I landed at Sally's. She greeted me with open arms when I knocked on the door. "Stay as long as you'd like," she said. Each night I lay on her couch with my eyes wide open, picturing one frightening scene after another. I would be so lonely. I couldn't recover from a divorce. I would never have the baby I so desperately wanted. I began to pray Tom would change his mind. I had seen plenty of movies where the husband left his wife, realized he had made a mistake, and begged her to let him come back. Maybe Tom would turn into one of these men. Even if he didn't call me tomorrow, he could still change his mind next week, next month, maybe even next year.

I woke up on my third morning on Sally's couch, knowing I had to go home and face what would now be my empty apartment. I tried to imagine the space without Tom. We had never talked about what he would take and leave behind.

When I got home, I put my key in the lock, feeling sick with dread and fear. Tom's side of the closet and his bureau drawers in the bedroom stood empty. The papers on his desk in his study were gone, and the bookshelf had been stripped bare. I sat down on the living room sofa. My eye went right to the middle of the floor, expecting to see the beloved Iranian coffee table. Tom, of course, had taken it, too.

CHAPTER 10

ELLEN

In the weeks after Tom left, the living room looked large and empty without the coffee table. I felt like a tiny girl sitting in a vast, dark cavern. The word "heartbroken," which had once seemed like an overwrought cliche from a romance novel, now couldn't capture the intensity of my grief. My heart was shattered, not just broken.

Sleep provided little relief. Each night I sat propped up in bed, thumbing through old copies of *Newsweek* magazine. At midnight I curled up on my side of the bed, piled several pillows on the spot where Tom used to sleep so I wouldn't feel so alone, and nodded off. Dreams of him jolted me awake three or four times during the night. At 4 am, I was up for good and stumbled into the kitchen. I boiled water for a cup of tea, took two bites of a toasted bagel, and dumped it in the garbage; everything I ate tasted like cardboard. I wandered into the living room, lay on the sofa, and cried.

My teaching semester had ended, and I had nothing to do. Occasionally, it occurred to me to be productive. I had just finished the first year of a two-year, temporary teaching position at Boston College. I had planned to turn my history dissertation into a book over the summer, knowing I wouldn't get a permanent, tenure track job without a publication. As much as I didn't want to lose my career on top of my husband, I couldn't force myself to sit at my desk and work; the part of my brain that had written a dissertation had shut down, possibly forever.

From the time Tom left, I hadn't done any laundry. On a Friday morning, I rummaged around a week's worth of dirty clothes on the bedroom floor, pulling out a rumpled t-shirt. I slid it over my head. Then I zipped up my stained jeans, so loose around my waist I needed to tighten my belt an extra notch. I stuffed some tissues in my pockets and headed for Joe's psychotherapy office. It would be my first session without Tom.

Joe was standing in the waiting room when I arrived. "I thought you forgot the appointment," he said, as his head tilted toward the clock. He sounded worried, and having someone even a little concerned about me felt comforting.

"I didn't realize I was late. I can't keep track of the time."

He followed me into his office. The room was quiet, apart from the soft hum of the white noise machine. We took the same seats we had had several weeks earlier, when Tom and I had that fateful marriage counseling appointment. I slumped down on the beige sofa. Joe sat on the comfortable blue chair. The bright sunlight streaming through the window hurt my eyes, and I turned my head away.

"How are you doing?" Joe said.

I tried to speak, but before I could get out a word, I started to cry. It wasn't gentle ladylike tears that ran down my cheeks.

These were loud, gasping sobs coming out of my mouth. I bent over, covered my face with my hands, and cried. Once or twice, I noticed Joe watching me with a worried look. He didn't say anything. I blew my nose, and almost immediately started crying again.

"I have never experienced this kind of pain before," I said.

Joe remained quiet. The room was still. He shifted in his seat and leaned forward. Then he placed his elbows on his knees, clasping his hands together. The expression on his face—brow furrowed, lips sloping downward, eyes looking directly into mine—looked so compassionate I felt like he was experiencing my emotional pain along with me.

"I didn't know grief could be this physical," I said. "My chest hurts the most. It feels like someone stabbed me with a large cleaver. I can't get the feeling to stop, no matter what I do." I pulled a tissue from the box and started crying again.

I stumbled over my first few words when I finally calmed down long enough to say something. Once I started talking about the pain of grief, I couldn't stop. With each new detail I provided Joe, his nod or soft "hmm" encouraged me to keep speaking. I peeked at the ticking clock on the wall behind him and realized I had been talking for twenty minutes straight.

I thought back to who I was before Tom left, a woman who was careful not to tell people too much about any unhappy feelings in case they felt as if I was burdening them. She had disappeared. I had become someone who answered the question "how are you?" with tears rolling down my cheeks and a blow-by-blow account of the story of my husband leaving me. Words tumbled out of my mouth, whether I wanted them to or not.

"I don't usually talk this much," I said. "Since Tom left, I just go on and on telling everyone how miserable I am."

"It's pretty normal," Joe said. "You probably feel like a dam burst inside you, and you can't stop the water from pouring out. People often feel this way in a crisis."

I paused for a few seconds and replayed Joe's words. I *did* feel like a bursting dam. He had captured my experience in a way I hadn't been able to articulate before, as if he completely understood me. Later, once I was training to become a therapist, I would learn that Joe's empathic response was the first step to create a bond between a therapist and patient that was conducive to healing. At this moment, however, I leaned back against the soft cushion of Joe's upholstered sofa and noticed how soothing it felt, making me think about my mom's cool hand against my fevered forehead when I was a little girl.

Suddenly, I glanced at the loveseat where Tom sat the last time I was here. As quickly as relief came into my mind, it went out, replaced by my memory of a conversation Tom and I had right before he left. "I asked Tom if he was going to miss me before he moved out," I said to Joe. "He said he wouldn't because he had too much work to do. It was excruciating to hear him say that."

I paused and tried to hold back my tears. It was no use. When I began to cry this time, the sobs were even louder than before. I sounded like a howling, wounded dog, caught in a trap.

"You must have been crushed," Joe said.

"Exactly. Crushed is the right word." Again, relief flooded me.

Although I didn't know it at the time, research would later suggest two reasons why a patient like myself felt relief from this type of therapeutic conversation. The psychologist Matthew

Lieberman noted that when people labeled a feeling with a word, the part of the brain involved in emotions, the amygdala, showed less activity, and the person calmed down. In the *Journal of Research in Personality*, Janetta Lun and her colleagues discovered that people who kept a mood diary reported feeling more satisfied with their lives when they believed people understood them. As I talked to Joe, these two experiences were happening at once. I put my feelings into words in the presence of someone who understood me. No wonder I felt relief.

I glanced at the clock and saw the session was almost over. "What are you going to do when you get home?" Joe asked.

"I'm just living minute to minute. Each hour of the day goes by so slowly. I read a little. I stare out the window. Toward the middle of the day, I turn on the TV and watch *The Young and the Restless.*"

Joe smiled. I smiled back at him for the first time since I'd sat down. He checked his watch. "I know this is a bad place to stop, but our time is almost up," he said.

I felt as if I had just sat down. How long had I been crying? This was a terrible place to stop, not just a bad one. I felt so comforted by Joe's reactions I wished I could stay curled on his sofa for the rest of the day. A thought entered my mind that would become a familiar one over the next six months: crying in therapy felt better than crying alone. Years later, this idea would inform my approach to my own patients who asked me how psychotherapy helps with grief. "It is good to have someone keep you company when you're grieving. It is better than facing a loss by yourself," I often said.

"Same time next week?" Joe asked.

"Yes," I said. I took a deep breath. I felt better than I did when I first sat down. If only the feeling could last longer than the fifty minutes I had spent with Joe. But the relief was fleeting. By the time I walked out his front door, I was crying all over again.

I didn't want to go home: more hours of soap operas, broken up by long crying jags. I needed to go somewhere other than my apartment. When I was young, I had spent many happy hours in the library with my mom. The library in the town where Joe had his office was only a few blocks away. I headed there, and as soon as I walked into the lobby, my shoulders relaxed.

I wandered down to the children's room and back up to the reference desk, passing the biographies and new fiction. Everywhere I looked people were doing exactly what I liked to do: read. It was so quiet here. Not the cold silence of my apartment. The library had a hushed silence of people turning the pages of their favorite books. Suddenly, I remembered the person I had been earlier in my life: the five-year-old sitting on the floor of the children's room with a book opened on her lap, the seventeen-year-old scribbling on her note cards at a desk in the New York Public Library, and the thirty-year-old roaming the stacks of the university library searching for books to help write a dissertation. I had come to a place that felt more like home than my empty apartment. Although I couldn't articulate this idea clearly at the time, this was the "me" I liked best: the reader, the researcher, and the student I had been for most of my life. I wasn't just a wife, for that matter a deserted one.

I climbed to the second floor, where the non-fiction books lined the shelves. I walked slowly down each aisle. The musty odor of old books made me relax even more. When I came to the history area, I lingered for a while, leafing through books I was familiar with and others I hoped to read one day. Then I wandered over to the psychology section. Little did I know, a year later, I would leave history behind and begin my training as a psychotherapist.

I wasn't searching for any particular book; I simply knew books had always provided me with direction in my life. One title grabbed my attention: *Crazy Time: Surviving Divorce and Building a New Life.* The author, Abigail Trafford, wrote the book after her divorce and had interviewed many men and women about their divorce experiences. I sat in one of the carrels and buried my head in the book, reading so carefully I felt like I was studying for an exam back in college. After I read Trafford's description of the abrupt emotional swings of divorce, I leaned back in my chair and felt as understood as I had with Joe only fifteen minutes earlier. The author's words mirrored my experience so closely I imagined she had written the book just for me. When I looked up at the clock, I realized twenty pain-free minutes had passed. At the library's closing time, I cradled *Crazy Time* in my arms and checked it out.

———

The following week I was back in Joe's office, sitting across from him on the beige sofa. The second—and then the third, and fourth—appointment was identical to the first. I described how grief-stricken I felt without Tom and sobbed throughout most of the session. Finally, Joe would make a comment that made me feel as if he understood me. By the time the hour was over, I felt better. Yet when I got out to my car, I would start crying all over again and continued on the drive back home.

By early July, eight weeks after Tom had left, I could get through more of the session without crying. I sat across from Joe one Friday afternoon, already knowing the topic I wanted to discuss. I told Joe that Tom was always on my mind. My conversations with Tom replayed in my brain no matter what I was doing: taking a shower, washing the dishes, trying to watch a show on TV. "It drives me crazy. I keep talking to him in my head," I said.

"What are you saying to him?" Joe asked.

"I'm defending myself, saying I'm not as bad as he made me out to be."

"Bad in what way?"

"All those things he said about me when we came to see you together," I said. "How I was selfish and inconsiderate." In these imaginary discussions, I presented myself in the best light. My desire to see plays, go to museums, and travel were all ways we could enjoy ourselves together and feel connected. "I just wanted to feel close to you," I pictured saying to Tom.

"He was the person who knew me best. If he thought something was wrong with me, he was probably right," I said to Joe, who listened to me with the same intensity I noticed during the previous sessions. His head turned toward mine. His eyes studied my face. Even the boys shouting outside his window didn't distract him from what I was saying. When I sighed, he sighed. Joe blinked a few times and roused himself from his focused concentration.

"Think about it a little. Tom had his own agenda," Joe said. "Everybody wants to look like a good guy when a marriage ends."

I nodded at Joe. Part of my brain noticed the similarity between his words and what Alexandra, my colleague, had said to me. They were both suggesting that the person who ended a relationship needed to make their partner's flaws the cause to assuage their own guilt. Had I been able to hold on to this perspective for more than a few seconds, I would have zipped through my sessions with Joe in record time, fully healed. Psychotherapy was far more complicated than that, I would discover several years later when I became a therapist. Insight, particularly early in the treatment, is a bright flash of light quickly covered up by long-standing personal struggles and the habitual ways in which a patient thinks.

I looked at Joe's clock, noticing it was time to go. The session had flown by again. I picked up my purse and drove home. As soon as I walked in the door, I switched on the TV; the sound of the voices was comforting. The afternoon dragged by, as it always did. Finally, the phone rang at night, and I knew it was a call from my parents, who had been worried about me since Tom left.

First, I talked to my mom, crying as I described the long, painful hours of my day. No matter where we started, I always brought the conversation back to the feeling I was responsible for the end of my marriage. "Tom left me because I was selfish," I said.

"That's not true," she said. "You are kind and understanding. It's *not your fault*." Her firm teacher's voice came through on the other end of the line; she would never tolerate anyone criticizing her daughter. My mother would then hand the phone to my dad.

I went over the same territory again, landing on my self-blame as I had done many times before. My father, quiet and thoughtful, would listen without saying anything for a while. "You know," he said, "people would rather take responsibility for a bad event than admit it was out of their control. Think about it. We'll call you tomorrow."

Wait a second, I thought, as the phone clicked off. My father seemed to be saying something similar to what Joe and even my colleague, Alexandra, had implied. That the blame I placed upon myself for the end of my marriage didn't make sense.

I turned off the TV, trying to clear my brain, but I still felt confused. My father's idea contradicted everything I believed about being an adult. I assumed adults made careful, thoughtful choices to ensure their lives turned out how they wanted, and I thought my father believed this, too. Why else would he have spent years telling me to think of the consequences of my decisions? "Look before you leap," he often said. Was he contradicting himself? Or, was the guidance he gave to the teenage version of me different from the advice he hoped the adult version of me would understand? Perhaps he wanted me to realize I couldn't control my life as much as I believed I could, no matter how much forethought I put into a decision. The outcome could still go awry.

My head was spinning. My brain had the buzzy feel of a wire short-circuiting. I glanced at the clock, thinking it would be another night with little sleep. I picked up *Crazy Time* again and opened it to where I had left off earlier. Divorce can make a woman feel she is about to lose her mind, the author wrote.

CHAPTER 11

MEGHAN

By mid-September, homework, tests, and parent–teacher conferences had taken over Meghan's life. Dressed in her professional attire, navy blue skirt and a carefully ironed blouse, she flew into my office right after school, the day's frustrations circling her mind. She loved teaching, she had told me many times. She liked watching her students' eyes light up when they finally understood a complicated math problem. Unfortunately, half the class didn't even do their homework. "It's disappointing," she said. "They don't seem to be learning as much as I hoped."

Her days felt long and complicated; "overwhelming" was the word she used. She ran from her school to her daughter's daycare to make sure she got there on time. Arriving at home twenty minutes later, they played peek-a-boo as Meghan made dinner. Then there was a bath, story time, and her daughter's lunch and snacks to be made for the next day. After she tucked her little girl into bed, Meghan would sit in front of her computer to focus on the next day's classes, yawning and struggling to stay awake. Unfortunately, Patrick still didn't help her as much as she wanted. "My friends tell me their husbands don't help out much either," she said one day. "That doesn't make me any less annoyed at Patrick."

Between life in constant motion and the couple's strained relationship, Meghan and Patrick seemed to be living in an uncomfortable truce. I pictured Patrick walking into the kitchen and Meghan walking out. I could hear the sharp, scraping sounds of their knives and forks against their plates as they ate in silence. I imagined the heavy tension in their house as they got ready for work each day, the way the summer air feels right before a thunderstorm, their conversation limited to "What time will you be home tonight?"

Meghan and Patrick had been seeing their marriage counselor for five months without any improvement. I thought of offering the name of a different counselor. There were plenty to choose from. The skyrocketing divorce rate had resulted in a growth in the number of people going into the profession, as the dramatic increase in membership of the American Association of Marriage and Family Therapists demonstrated over the past fifty years. Who would I recommend? Which theory of marriage counseling would be well suited to their problem? I considered the one I knew best, the work of psychologist John Gottman.

Gottman recognized that people in troubled marriages argued in destructive ways. They attacked each other's personality, acted defensively, displayed disdain toward their partner, and my ex-husband's favorite, refused to say anything, "stonewalling" as Gottman called it. He suggested that couples who resorted to these negative behaviors had a ninety percent chance of divorcing. Still, they could improve their marriages by learning more positive ways to disagree with one another, such as calming down before they spoke and explaining their view to their partner without blame.

I liked Gottman's common sense approach and relied on it frequently when I saw couples. Yet as I had often discovered as a therapist, implementing a theory proved more difficult than I anticipated. Teaching a couple a new way to argue was easier said than done. The desire from one partner to prove the other wrong, have the last word, or unload a long history of resentments, fueled the fire and accelerated fights rather than extinguished them. Sometimes, when I worked with couples who couldn't stop screaming at each other, I pictured myself running out of my office and leaving them sitting there alone.

I tried to figure out how Meghan and Patrick would do with a therapist like Gottman. They didn't sound like screamers. Nevertheless, there was no way to compromise about having another child, even if they had calm discussions. If they didn't have a second kid, Meghan would be unhappy; if they had one, Patrick would be resentful.

Meghan interrupted my train of thought. "Patrick and I decided to stop marriage counseling," she said.

"You don't want to try someone else?"

"No," she said. Instead, they would concentrate on individual therapy. She would continue to see me, and Patrick would get his own therapist.

Meghan wanted to use individual therapy to understand herself better, and I thought that was a great idea. She had spent years trying to figure out Patrick. It was a hard habit to break. Yet, despite her decision to work on herself, she spent much of the session telling me stories about her husband. Their one trip to

England failed because Patrick turned out to be uncomfortable in a foreign country, often grabbing her hand like a frightened little boy. He was so timid, she complained. A week later, she launched into a story about Patrick's constant gripes about his job. He had worked at the same marketing company for five years, disliking it the whole time. "He never bothers to look for a new job," she said. "I don't understand him."

For the next fifteen minutes, she talked about how hard Patrick took his parents' divorce. "I worried about him," she said. "He didn't seem to be able to manage his life by himself." I imagined Patrick's divorcing parents screaming as Meghan swooped in, like a mother bird, and saved him. Only ten years later could she see the cost of her constant supervision. "I took over doing so much in his life he never had to learn how to do things on his own," she said.

"It sounds like a statement a parent would make about a son, not the kind a wife would make about her husband," I said. I watched her face, waiting to see where she would go from here. I hoped we were done with Patrick. After all, Meghan had spent their whole married life trying to smooth the way for him. Now it was time to focus on what she wanted. Nonetheless, she circled back to him again. My foot jiggled up and down as if it were impatiently waiting to tap Meghan on her shoe. I wanted her to stop analyzing Patrick's life and start asking questions about her own. "Sorry to interrupt," I finally said. This was the line I always used to encourage a patient to talk about a different topic, the one I believed to be more important than the one they were discussing. "How would you feel if your life didn't include Patrick?"

Meghan was quiet and looked down at the floor. "I don't know," she said. "I don't usually think much about my feelings."

"How come?"

"I don't feel comfortable talking about them," she said.

I took a second look at Meghan and noticed something I hadn't recognized before: her face revealed little about her feelings. Her forehead remained smooth, and her eyes didn't narrow as I expected when she talked about her anger at Patrick. I wondered if she was embarrassed about expressing her emotions or even fearful about acknowledging them to herself.

I understood this fear all too well, thinking about the uneasiness I felt the night before my wedding. Then there were the many other feelings I had ignored during my marriage: the hurt when Tom teased me, the disappointment at how distant we had become from one another. Later it became clear to me that I pretended these feelings didn't exist to maintain the marriage. Meghan might be doing the same thing.

Feelings can be amorphous, embarrassing, messy, and even contradictory. They don't necessarily match the person we believe ourselves to be. An image of Meghan, the teacher, standing at the whiteboard working through a math problem came into my mind; maybe she didn't try to identify her feelings because they couldn't be easily tabulated. I needed more information to get to the bottom of her problematic relationship with her own emotions.

"What messages did your parents give about feelings?" I asked.

"None," she said. "None at all. They never talked about feelings."

Her father approached her problems logically. He skipped right to the solution without considering how she felt. Her mom never encouraged Meghan to express herself when she was upset. Both her mom and dad wanted Meghan to find an answer to the issue and move on. In an article entitled, "Parental Socialization of Emotions," Nancy Eisenberg and her colleagues found that parents who disapproved of their children's expressions of emotion conveyed the message that feelings were threatening. Consequently, the youngster didn't learn how to explore the meaning of her feelings nor how to manage them. Meghan's emotional life likely remained a mystery to her for that very reason.

"Emotions are the body's way of warning us about dangers or telling us about the pleasure we can have in our lives," I said. "It is hard to make a decision if you can't recognize what you feel."

I went on to tell Meghan about the research of the psychologist Antonio Damasio. He discovered that people with lesions in a region of the brain processing emotions—the orbital cortex, the prefrontal cortex, and the amygdala—had difficulty making decisions. Because these people could still think logically, they could weigh the costs and benefits of two possible options. When choosing a restaurant, for example, they could compare the pluses and minuses of restaurant A, with better prices, to restaurant B, which was closer to home. However, their brain lesions impaired their ability to experience the emotions that would tell them what food they wanted. Consequently, they struggled for hours trying to decide which restaurant to choose.

"Here's the moral of the story," I said. "You have to know what you feel about Patrick and your marriage to decide about your future. It is not just a rational calculation of the pros and cons of staying married versus getting divorced."

"How do I figure out what I feel?" she asked.

"Sometimes, it is easier to identify an emotion if you focus on different parts of your body. For example, does your gut churn when you have to talk to your boss? If so, what word would you put to the churning: fear, worry, dread? Or do the muscles in your neck feel tight, and what label would you give to this tightness? Frustration or irritation, perhaps. After a while, you will get better at checking in with yourself to figure out what you feel."

Megan scrunched up her forehead.

"Just try it during the week and see what you discover. The goal is to identify your feelings without worrying about whether the emotion is right or wrong."

I wondered what she would find. A pain in her chest as she started to grieve for a marriage on its last legs? Dread in her stomach about a decision she didn't want to make? Burning in her cheeks when she finally acknowledged if she left Patrick, she would inevitably hurt him and her daughter?

After Meghan left my office, I picked up my pen to write in her chart. I tried to figure out how best to describe her difficulty expressing her emotions. I recalled the story she told me about the other man she had been interested in—another teacher at her school. He appealed to her enough she considered leaving Patrick. Yet, in the end, she discounted her interest in him as a sign of immaturity. She convinced herself a reasonable adult would continue on the path she had forged for herself: teaching career, marriage, house buying, and pregnancy. I wondered if her desire to meet appropriate social expectations, what she *should* do, in other words, made it difficult for her to know her heart.

I jotted down a few notes and stopped to think about Meghan's view of adulthood. It centered on the steps a young person should take on the path toward growing up. I pictured a young woman marching along through her twenties, achieving one milestone after another. Like notches on a belt, I thought. Or checking off the boxes, as Meghan called it. The fact she might never have a second child disrupted her expectations about her adult achievements. There could be something more here as well. I imagined her tiptoeing towards a new view of adulthood entirely. She would no longer live her life meeting one goal after another; she would consider what she *wanted* to do, where her feelings took her, not simply what she *ought* to do.

In the subsequent few sessions, Meghan's view of Patrick and her marriage vacillated. First she would voice a complaint about him. Then, almost immediately, she did an about-face, reassuring me he was a good guy.

"It's normal to be uncertain about what to do," I said.

Meghan could only remain paralyzed for so long, trying to balance Patrick's negative qualities against his positive ones. Soon, his flaws dominated the conversation. At one point, I commented on her change of heart, watching her to see if she would reconsider. Maybe Patrick wasn't as bad as she made him out to be? Had I been the marriage therapist, I would have pressed her harder. After all, focusing on your spouse's flaws, to the exclusion of their assets, would not make a marriage happy. Meghan, however, hadn't come to me to find a way to improve her relationship with her husband. Whether or not I thought she should try to save the marriage was beside the point. She hoped I could help her identify what she really wanted in her life.

I compared my approach to Meghan's therapy with that of my patient Lisa. Lisa struggled with self-doubt and needed a therapist to point out the strengths she didn't know she had. Meghan exuded confidence, displaying her take-charge attitude about her life. She needed a psychotherapist to help her accept her confusion and encourage her to explore her heart.

I had been a therapist long enough to understand Meghan's increasing dissatisfaction with her husband. Patrick's initial reluctance to have another child had opened the door for her to think about her marriage differently. I imagined her as a little Dutch boy pulling his finger out of the dike, rather than sticking it in as he did in the Hans Brinker story. Once she considered the possibility her marriage wouldn't work, the many compromises she had made along the way no longer seemed acceptable to her, and dissatisfied feelings flooded in. It was as if she were rewriting the history of her marriage, so her husband's quirks, which she had previously lived with comfortably, now looked like flaws she could barely tolerate.

Was her current, disappointing version of the marriage more accurate than her earlier happy one? No. But it wasn't any less accurate either. Both served a purpose. As Meghan changed—from a reasonably satisfied married woman to an unhappy one—her stories needed to change, too. Each one helped her make sense of who she was and who she was trying to become. When she finally decided what to do about her marriage, which version of Meghan would she turn out to be?

CHAPTER 12

LISA

When Greg refused to leave his job, Lisa realized her needs mattered little to him. He wanted her back, but only on his terms. She refused to buy into those terms any longer. She was done with marriage counseling, she told me. She would continue meeting with me for individual therapy until she decided on her next step. As much as I thought she should divorce Greg, my job would be to sit back and let Lisa take the time she needed to reach a decision.

She leaned forward in the chair in early December and talked about the upcoming holiday. She looked so sad. "I am going to celebrate Christmas without Greg," she said. "It will be the first holiday without him since we married."

For the past thirty years, she, Greg, and their kids had gone to his parents' house every Christmas. All of his siblings and their offspring showed up there. I tried to picture the scene. The rich scent of roasted turkey floated from the kitchen into the living room, followed by the pungent smell of the garlic in the paella. Greg's family was Spanish, and his mom was a talented cook. I imagined the grandparents, aunts, uncles, and cousins gathering around the dining room table, laughing and clinking glasses of red wine as they talked, just like in a Hollywood movie.

A week ago, Greg called her and said she could still come to his parents' house. Lisa felt pulled in two different directions. The thought of seeing her husband, much less at a family get-together, turned her stomach. Yet she had been close to her in-laws through the years and loved celebrating Christmas with them. When she thought about splitting up with Greg, she worried she would lose her in-laws, too. She was right. This could be a likely scenario. Like tiny tribes, families huddled around their own and excluded the outsider, the in-law. Still, I wondered whether her connection to Greg's family might survive a divorce. Everyone knew about his affair and disapproved.

What about Lisa's family? Were they helping her through this challenging time? I remembered the relief I felt when my parents called me nightly, right after Tom left. Maybe Lisa's parents were different from mine.

"What about your family?" I asked.

She was closer to Greg's family than her own.

"How did that happen?"

Lisa's parents divorced years ago. Her dad and his wife lived in North Carolina, and Lisa saw little of them. Her mom lived close by, as did her sister. Before she and Greg split up, Lisa would ask him to have the occasional holiday meal with her family. "Boring" was the word he used to describe an afternoon with her mom and sister. "They are too quiet," he said. He wanted Christmas, Easter, and even July 4th with his family. Lisa went along with him. Over time, the ties between her and her own family frayed. As I listened to her talk, I wondered if she realized how much she had given up for her husband.

"Maybe if you don't stay with Greg, you will become closer to your own family," I said.

She paused for a few seconds before launching into another discussion about Greg's family. Every year, right before Christmas, Lisa ate lunch in a restaurant with her mother-in-law and sisters-in-law. "Now that Greg and I are separated, I don't know if I'm still invited," she said. Her voice trailed off into a whisper.

I thought back to my divorce. After Tom left, my grief felt like an onion. Each day I would peel back another layer and discover something new I had lost. First, he disappeared. His family went next. I gave up our apartment because I couldn't afford to live there alone. Within a year, I also lost my career as a historian; without Tom to support me, I couldn't keep searching for a university teaching position.

Lisa looked defeated, and I struggled to find the right words to say. "You can always call your mother-in-law and ask if it is okay if you come," I said, thinking about how much direct, plain advice I doled out to patients. This advice had nothing to do with any particular psychotherapeutic theory, and sometimes it made me feel like a practical grandmother suggesting a common-sense solution to a problem. It turned out to be not what Lisa needed, however.

"I guess so," she said. She paused, looked out my office window, and back at me.

"What is it?" I asked.

"The way Greg treated me made me feel so rejected and worthless. I don't want to take a chance his family might reject me, too."

I slowed down and studied Lisa's face. Her eyes were watery and wide. I had overlooked how vulnerable she felt in my rush to be helpful. Every therapist makes a mistake like this one at some point in their career. Misunderstanding a patient early in the therapy—when the person doesn't know if the therapist is trustworthy—could cause her to terminate treatment abruptly. Since I knew Lisa well by now, an apology would be sufficient. "I'm sorry I didn't understand how scary this is for you," I said. "Remember, your mother-in-law promised to remain close. I doubt they will reject you. Just skip lunch this year, if it is easier."

The upcoming holiday made Lisa think about her grown daughter and sons. "What will my kids do for Christmas if I don't go to Greg's family?" she said. "Will they go without me?" She had never celebrated the holiday without them. "I really wish they decide to spend Christmas with me. I'll be hurt if they don't."

She felt torn. A big part of her wanted to ask them to give up their usual Christmas tradition and stay home with her. She pictured the three of them lounging in their pajamas around the Christmas tree, cups of steaming hot chocolate in their hands. It sounded like a scene Norman Rockwell could have painted. On the other hand, another part knew her kids should make their decision independently, and she didn't want to put them in the middle between her and Greg.

Through my years as a therapist, I saw many separated and divorced patients whose anger at their former partner spilled onto their children. Lisa was different. She never uttered a bad word about Greg to her kids, no matter how angry she became.

If only Caroline, a fifty-year-old former patient of mine, had a spouse who was similarly determined to make children's lives easy during a separation. Caroline's ex-husband was the opposite. Incensed she had left him, he fed their fourteen-year-old daughter a steady stream of demeaning comments about her mom until the girl refused to visit Caroline on the weekends. Parental alienation syndrome is the psychiatric term to describe what happened to this teenager.

"It's normal to want the children to be on your side. Just don't act on the impulse," I told Lisa.

Christmas is tough on families when parents live in two different homes. Inevitably, the choice about where to celebrate brings up the issue of loyalty even for adults. I thought about a conversation I had several years earlier with thirty-five-year-old Jessica. She was married with a three-year-old boy, and her parents had been separated since Jessica was a baby. Despite the decades that had gone by, she spent the weeks leading up to the holiday worrying about where she should go for Christmas. "My father is picky. He doesn't want toy trucks and cars strewn around his living room like we have in our house. It makes it difficult to be there." Still he would be hurt if she spent Christmas with her mom. The solution ended up being difficult for her. On Christmas day, she drove an hour north of Boston to see her mom in the morning and then went south of the city, another two-hour trip, to see her dad. Several months later, an image of Jessica's scowling face came back to me when I saw the newspaper headline, "Never Too Old to Hurt From Parents' Divorce."

The impending holiday made Lisa realize her split from Greg would alter many aspects of her family. Her crushed face brought to mind Penny, another former patient who summed up this experience better than anyone I ever met. She had divorced her husband ten years earlier when her kids were twelve, thirteen, and seventeen. "I knew leaving my ex-husband was the right thing to do. I hoped it would be better for my children because they wouldn't have to live with parents who frequently yelled at each other," she said. "I can remember the sorrowful look on their faces the day I told them Ed and I were getting divorced. I had this image of a happy family I wanted them to have."

"Like a Hallmark greeting card," I said.

She nodded. "It was my choice to leave their father, and I caused them the kind of pain I never wanted them to feel," she said. "The heartache I felt at hurting them has never gone away. After ten years, I doubt it ever will."

Divorce had shattered Penny's image of the happy family she hoped to give her kids. Before Greg's affair, Lisa had held on to her own version of this picture. "You know," she said. "When my daughter was born, I swore I would never get divorced, so she wouldn't have to go through what I did, growing up."

"Like what?" I asked.

"I was a young teenager when I suspected my father was having an affair. It is hard to remember what gave me that impression. Maybe it was just that he came home late many nights. Or maybe I heard my parents in their bedroom arguing about it. It was a terrible time in my life."

Now her children were facing almost the identical experience she had encountered: a father who had had an affair and parents on the verge of divorce. She looked crushed. "I couldn't prevent my kids from going through exactly what I didn't want them to go through."

It took me a few seconds to decide what to say. "When you made the promise to stay married, you didn't know you would end up with a husband who was repeatedly unfaithful," I said. "The Greg you married thirty years ago differs from the Greg you are married to today. I doubt you would choose this new Greg as a friend, much less as a husband."

Before I went on, I checked Lisa's face to see how this had landed. She looked like she was concentrating hard. So far so good. "Promises are easy to make when you are young. Now you realize marriage can be more complicated than you ever imagined." I hoped my words resonated with her. If they didn't ring a bell today, she might remember them later, years from now, when we were no longer seeing each other. Psychotherapy sometimes works this way.

We had another ten minutes left in the session, and Lisa stayed focused on her daughter and sons. "I feel like my kids don't really have a family anymore if I divorce Greg." I imagined the kind of Christmas card she probably sent out before Greg's affair: a photo of the family smiling with their arms draped over one another. Next year Greg would be missing from the picture. I hoped soon Lisa would see the new kind of family she would have with her kids wasn't necessarily broken, as divorced families are often called, simply rearranged.

"You and your kids will still be part of a family," I said. "It will just be a different kind than you imagined for them."

Lisa didn't say anything. She shrugged her shoulders.

"It might take some time for you to see it. After a while, you will have different traditions for your new kind of family, recent memories of places you went and activities you enjoyed together."

Before she left my office, Lisa said she would go to her mom's house for Christmas. She looked defeated, as if she was imagining a holiday dinner where she, her mom and her sister would be eating their dry turkey in silence. Her kids would likely stay with tradition and go to Greg's parents' house.

––––––––––

Lisa came in for her next appointment in early January. "What did you end up doing for the holiday?" I asked her, as soon as she sat down.

She had gone to her mom's house for Christmas dinner. Her sister came, too, and they had eaten roast beef, not turkey, and exchanged gifts. It was low-key but still fun.

"You sound surprised," I said.

"Yes, I never really gave it a chance before."

"Maybe a quiet get-together suits you more than you realized," I said, thinking of Greg as a man who liked a life filled with flash and razzamatazz. Lisa seemed to enjoy simpler pleasures. She gave me a quick nod, but she was ready to move on to another topic. Before we did, I wanted to make sure she realized the significance of her decision to spend the holiday without her husband and children. As a therapist, I often plant tiny seeds that might not take root for weeks or even months. "Having Christmas without Greg was a big accomplishment," I said.

"I guess so," she said. "By the way, I've decided to stop returning Greg's phone calls and texting him back."

"Baby steps," I said, borrowing a line from the shrink in the film *What About Bob?*

"What's it like not to return his text?" I asked.

She sat up straight, and a sly grin played at the corners of her mouth. "At first, it felt rude. Then I realized I'm not required to answer him." The grin spread into a wide smile across her face. "Greg hates to be ignored."

CHAPTER 13

ELLEN

"**S**top at the bank," I mumbled to myself as I drove home from Joe's office. Yet my foot remained glued to the gas pedal, and I sailed right past the Harvard Trust, where Tom and I had our accounts. We had had one discussion about money before he left. "You keep the savings account," he said. "I'll take the new car." That was eight weeks ago, and I still hadn't changed our joint account to an individual one; either of us could make a withdrawal whenever we wanted. One day soon, I would have to stop at the bank. I couldn't face the problem right now.

I was eating a peanut butter and jelly sandwich at the kitchen table for dinner when my parents phoned. Right away, my dad steered the conversation around to money. I wasn't surprised; my parents had been young during the Great Depression, and the specter of financial insecurity had always hovered above their heads. Later on, I would understand he was looking into a future I was too focused on the present to see. Both of us knew my teaching contract would only run for another year. After that, I would be unemployed in a job market with few academic openings for historians. At the time, I was too worried about my emotional survival to worry about my financial one.

"Change the bank account from a joint one to your own. Don't put it off," my father said. The implication was clear. If you don't cut off Tom's access to the bank account, you might not have any money. "The money is yours. Just take it."

I was worried about making a move on my own. Tom might disapprove if I took charge of our bank account. Perhaps he would need some cash, and he wouldn't be able to get it. "It's not your problem," my father would say. I thought about Tom getting mad about money, and the old feeling of dread in the face of his icy anger resurfaced. But he told me the money was mine; it was *my* account now, not *ours*.

All night long, I sat in the living room and considered the angles of what I thought was a significant dilemma. Tom had moved all his things out. He had told me our marriage was over. Yet I felt disloyal, dishonest even, changing the bank account without telling him. He might think I had stolen money from him.

I would have felt less alone that night had I known of Olivia, who became one of my psychotherapy patients years later, once I switched careers. After her husband, Tony, left her and moved in with his girlfriend, her mom had to drive her to the bank to set up an individual account. She was as scared as I was to take charge of her finances. "I believed Tony when he told me I wasn't good at handling money," she said. "My hand was shaking when I signed the signature card to open an individual account."

It would take me months to understand my lack of self-confidence more clearly: my identity as a married woman hadn't yet loosened its grip. No wonder I couldn't make a decision without considering how Tom would react. It was as if the seven years of marriage had left me unable to think independently. I didn't yet feel single, free to make any financial decisions on my own.

I paced back and forth between the living room and the bedroom. Then I lay down in bed and stared at the ceiling. The bedroom window was open wide, and a soft breeze blew in. I stretched out on the king-size bed, taking over the entire space. A lovely night, I thought. The constant chatter in my mind quieted as I concentrated on the silence. Tom did not live in my home anymore, I repeated to myself. He was not part of my life. He wasn't coming back, and I didn't need to think about his feelings any longer. I could make any decision I wanted without consulting him. Then I closed my eyes and, for the first time in weeks, I fell right to sleep.

I headed out to the bank the next day. As soon as I arrived, I walked to the bank manager's desk and waited for her to finish a phone call, butterflies in my stomach. Finally, she hung up and tugged at her suit jacket to straighten it out. She looked at me and stuck out her hand to shake mine.

"I need to change my joint account to an individual one," I said.

"Why are you making the change?" she asked.

I hadn't anticipated the question, and my eyes filled with tears. When I glanced at her, I saw how worried she looked. She pointed to the chair next to her desk. I sat down with tears running down my cheeks. I dug into my purse and rummaged around, hoping to find a tissue that didn't look like I had fished it out of the trash.

"My husband just left me," I replied.

In my life before Tom moved out, I would have stopped there, adhering to the norm of social conversations with strangers: don't spill your guts out to them. Now I seemed unable to stop. For the next ten minutes, I told her my entire divorce story.

She said, "Oh, no." Her head bobbed up and down in a sympathetic nod. She smiled at me. "I'm divorced, too," she said when I got to the end of my story.

I felt relieved, imagining an invisible thread connecting us. The bank manager handed me a pen and pushed over the papers to sign. No questions asked. Like that, I was now a woman in charge of her own money.

On the drive home, I pictured the bank manager as another new friend who understood what it was like to go through a divorce. Then I added her name to the number of people I was keeping track of in my head. My friend Sally and her partner Warren were both divorced. Cara, whose husband had left her for another woman the previous year, had to go on the list. Then, of course, there was Abigail Trafford, the author of *Crazy Time*, and the many men and women she interviewed for her book.

I wasn't really surprised at the length of my list. In the 1980s I would have had to have been a hermit not to realize how frequently people split up with their spouses. Marital instability had already become a popular theme in books, television shows, and movies. In the seven years Tom and I had been married, new films with plots revolving around divorce came out every month: *An Unmarried Woman*, *Kramer vs. Kramer*, *Scenes From a Marriage*. Newspapers and magazines were filled with articles on the subject. In July 1981 a *New York Times* piece declared that divorce was so prevalent any marriage, even a long, seemingly solid one, could dissolve without warning. Researchers pointed out that fifty percent of marriages in the early 1980s ended in divorce.

No matter how many newspaper articles on divorce I had read, no matter how many movies I had watched, the unraveling of my own marriage still stunned me. Naively, I had assumed it wouldn't happen to me. Later, I realized my view of marriage was a hold-over from the world I grew up in, where each house on my suburban road contained a neat nuclear family: mother and father and their children. My family was like that, too. Of course, I was too young to consider what these marriages were really like. Somehow or other I hadn't moved along with the times, imagining my marriage would turn out like my parents' which had lasted for forty years.

———

By late afternoon, the early July day had turned into a scorcher. When I opened the living room window, I heard my next-door neighbor, Mary, playing outside with her young daughter. Up to this point, I had successfully avoided her. An uneasy feeling took over as I imagined talking to her.

Why was I scared? Mary was friendly and warm with a wide Midwestern smile. We had chatted over the fence separating our backyards many times. But I knew where the conversation would lead. First, we would talk about how big her daughter had grown. Next, one of us would comment on the beautiful weather we had been having. Finally, she would ask me the question she always asked: how's your husband?

I feared a repeat of my conversation with the bank manager; I would try to offer a brief version of my split with Tom, only to have all the painful details gush out of my mouth. I also worried about how Mary would react to my news.

Why was I worried? The stigma once associated with divorce was disappearing; after all, Americans had elected Ronald Reagan, a man who had been divorced, as president. Nonetheless, the way in which people used the words "failed marriage" interchangeably with the word divorce made me embarrassed to tell Mary that Tom had left me. If she asked me what happened, I might end up admitting not only had my marriage failed but I had failed to notice it was failing. Before Tom left, I had considered myself an insightful woman. A divorce wouldn't have blindsided that type of woman; she would have recognized her marriage was unraveling.

Embarrassment barely scratched the surface of what I was feeling. Humiliation seemed like the more accurate word, worming its way into my brain, making me avoid Mary. Perhaps she would frown. Or give me a sideways glance when I told her Tom left me. Would she speculate about what I had done to Tom to *make* him leave? Years later, when I became a psychotherapist, I realized Mary had become the person on whom I projected my sense of humiliation. On this hot July afternoon, however, all I did was sit on the sofa, worrying as I listened to Mary and her daughter giggle together.

To some degree, the author of *Crazy Time* had prepared me for this moment. Abigail Trafford devoted a full chapter to the difference between the private divorce and the public one. The private divorce was my personal struggle with feelings of sadness, confusion, and fear. The public divorce would be the community's reaction to the news about the end of my marriage. A month after Tom's departure, all my close friends and family members—my immediate community—knew what had happened, and all of them offered their support. I hadn't, however, spoken to Mary since the winter, the last season I believed I was happily married, and I feared she would disapprove of me when I gave her the news.

There was another issue playing into my desire to avoid Mary, which was hard to acknowledge at the time. I was jealous of her. When she first moved next door to me, I noticed our differences. She and her husband Paul had come to Boston so he could enroll in graduate school, and she stayed home to take care of her two girls. Though she was only two years older than me, Mary seemed old-fashioned. Just a housewife, I thought. In contrast, I saw myself as a more modern woman, a feminist finishing a graduate degree and preparing to be a college professor.

I always felt like I had made better choices about my life than she had. At this moment though, many of my choices seemed like mistakes. For all my feminist thinking, Mary, the 1950s throw-back, looked like she was going to end up with what I desperately wanted for myself: a loyal husband and kids.

I didn't want to spend the rest of the afternoon peering at Mary through the window. I screwed my courage up, walked out the door, and said hello. "Not well," I said when she asked me how I was. I filled her in on the last difficult few weeks of my life. She offered a warm, sympathetic smile, not the squinty, sideways look I expected. As I watched her, I thought of the bank manager who had been so understanding earlier in the day. Both women would come to mind a month later, when a friend of a friend, a woman I barely knew, and her boyfriend showed up at my apartment to help me move out.

Several days later, I heard a sharp rap on my front door. I wasn't expecting anyone in the middle of the afternoon. I opened the door to a man in a suit and tie who looked like a Jehovah's Witness. Yet somehow the sober look on his face made me think of someone attending a funeral, not an enthusiastic young person doing God's work. He wasn't holding a Bible in his hand either. The neatly dressed man gripped his briefcase in one hand and some papers in the other.

He smiled at me and told me his name. I said hello, still confused about why he had come to my front door. He explained he was a constable. I was still smiling but my stomach started to feel queasy. A constable? Had I done something wrong? No, he was at my door to serve me with divorce papers.

"Divorce papers?" I asked.

The constable's eyes drifted away from mine as if he were trying to teleport himself back to his office. Nonetheless, he was there to do a job, and he did it efficiently. He handed me the paper, nodded his head, and thanked me. As fast as he could, he backed down the steps, turned around and drove away.

I was shocked. I had assumed Tom would take his time before he filed for divorce. At the least, he could have called to warn me the papers were coming. Would that have been too much to ask? I shut the door and trudged into my apartment, feeling like I was dragging a fifty-pound weight behind me.

I sat on the sofa and spread the paper out on my lap. The form was called Complaint for Divorce. On the top of the page, an official from the court had typed Tom's name as the plaintiff and mine as the defendant. "The defendant" sounded like someone who had committed a crime. I certainly felt guilty about many of the accusations Tom had thrown at me. It would take me many months to realize my only crime had been marrying the wrong man.

My eyes ran down the form and skidded to a halt at the line where each of our addresses was supposed to be. Mine was the apartment we had lived in together and where I still lived. Tom's address was a post office box in the town where he taught college. Just when I thought there was nothing more he could do to surprise me, this one small detail buried me under an avalanche of pain. Only a man who believed his wife had ruined his life would take this step to conceal where he lived from her. This new kind of rejection, again one I hadn't anticipated, made me feel as if my husband had slapped me in the face. Of course, there were other less sinister reasons why Tom kept his address from me—perhaps he hadn't found a permanent home—although these explanations would only occur to me months later. At the time I could only see the dark meaning of his post office box. Divorcing me wasn't enough. He needed to purge me from his life. When Tom first left, I imagined him disappearing from our marriage. Now it felt like he was disappearing from the planet.

I tried to pull myself together and figure out what I was supposed to do now. My mind raced through all the divorcing couples in movies I had seen over the past ten years, landing on Dustin Hoffman, playing Ted Kramer, in the film *Kramer vs. Kramer*. The confusion on his face after his wife left him mirrored mine. I couldn't remember whether or not he had sought legal help immediately. "Tomorrow," I said to myself. "I will look for an attorney tomorrow."

CHAPTER 14

ELLEN

All week long, I looked forward to another therapy appointment. As I drove to Joe's office on a hot July day, part of me felt embarrassed that the psychotherapy sessions were still so important in my life. I wished I was further along in my recovery. I had made *some* progress. There were clean clothes, neatly folded in my bedroom bureau rather than piled in a heap on the floor. I no longer spent each day crying and watching soap operas on TV. Instead, I had a created routine for myself: up at 7 am for a lap swim at the YMCA, regular trips to the grocery store, and three meals a day. Nonetheless, my progress still moved at a snail's pace; a day where I barely thought about Tom was followed by a day where he was all I could think about.

Nights were the worst. Without any distractions, unanswered questions bombarded my brain. How did I end up being blindsided by Tom? Had I lived with my head in the sand for seven years? What should I change about myself to prevent a similar situation from happening in the future? A lot was riding on my figuring out where I had gone wrong. At some point, I would want to have another serious relationship, and I still yearned for a baby. I wouldn't trust myself to try again with another man until I understood my mistakes in my marriage.

Joe's footsteps made a light tapping sound as he walked down the corridor to the waiting area where I sat. He popped his head around the corner and said, "hello." When we walked into his office, he took his regular seat on the blue chair, and I sat on the beige sofa, as I did every week. He leaned back in his chair, smiled, and waited without saying anything.

It had taken me two or three therapy sessions to get used to his initial silence. At first, I fidgeted in my seat and considered breaking the ice with comments about the weather. Then, at the end of the first month of therapy, I understood the purpose of his silence: it freed me up to talk about whatever was on my mind. On the drive over here, I had already decided where to start today.

"If someone had asked me if my marriage was happy during those seven years I lived with Tom, I would have said yes. I can't believe it now."

Joe nodded, and I kept going. "In the month before Tom left, I thought we were at such a good place in our lives. We both had full-time jobs and were earning more money than ever. We were planning to start a family. Whatever problems we had seemed normal ones to me. I didn't think Tom and I were having the kind of difficulties that break up a couple."

Joe nodded again.

"How did I get everything so wrong?" I asked.

"Maybe you weren't paying attention to the right things," he said.

"What should I have been paying attention to?"

"You were looking at the external aspects of your life. Maybe you didn't think enough about the internal factors. Your feelings, Tom's feelings."

The word "feelings" stirred something in me. "Even though I believed I was happy in my marriage, I also felt jittery and anxious much of the time," I said. The nervousness differed from the keyed-up feeling before an exam, which made sense, and disappeared as soon as the test was over. The uneasiness I felt was always in the background and didn't seem to have a cause. I could never fully relax. "Here is the weird thing," I said. "I haven't had the feeling since Tom moved out."

Joe explained anxiety could mask other feelings. For example, an individual facing a challenging situation might ignore her emotional reactions. She might even be trying to avoid the feelings. Yet they remained in her body, transformed into anxiety. "Perhaps your negative feelings about your marriage lurked in the back of your brain and turned into some kind of nervousness."

I struggled to take this in. Had I been anxious in my marriage without being aware of it? Did this anxiety cover up complicated feelings that would have warned me my marriage wasn't as happy as I thought it was? Which feelings were I trying to ignore?

"Here is something I noticed," Joe said. "You rarely talk about being angry at Tom. Most people whose husbands have walked out on them are mad."

My face felt warm and tight. I looked out Joe's window and then over his shoulder at the books on his desk. I studied a box of red, white, and blue Lego in the corner of the room. I shifted around on the chair before I said anything.

"Anger makes me uncomfortable. It's an emotion I can't control."

"Didn't you ever get mad at Tom?" Joe asked.

"Sure. Then I realized there was always a price to pay. When I got angry, he stopped speaking to me. So, I kept it inside until I was alone. Then I lost it."

"What happened?"

"About four years ago, he was upset because I had been complaining about how hard it was to write my dissertation. Maybe I *had* talked his ear off. But he had ignored me for three days, and I kept thinking whatever I had done wasn't bad enough to deserve this kind of punishment."

I just wanted Tom to say something to me. Anything. The silence was making me nuts. Yet every time I tried to catch his eye, he looked away. One day, after he left for class, I paced from the kitchen into the living room and back again. The anger built up slowly, and I felt a pounding in my head that wouldn't let up. I glanced at the clock, calculating Tom wouldn't be home for at least another hour. I sat down at the kitchen table and ran my hand over the smooth wood finish. Then I grabbed the edge, flipped it over, and heard the loud crash it made when it hit the floor.

"I felt like I had turned into a crazy woman," I said. "I stared at the table on the floor, shocked by what I had done."

Immediately, I squatted down, grabbed one of the table legs, and tugged on it. It was heavier than I realized, and I struggled for a few minutes. When I finally pulled it up, I was ashamed of losing control of my temper.

Joe frowned. "You didn't realize the dynamic between you and Tom was a recipe for getting out of control. He stopped speaking. You got angry. He still wouldn't talk to you. You felt helpless which fueled your anger even more," Joe said. "I understand why you threw the table over."

"I never thought about my anger that way," I said. "I thought something was wrong with me because I couldn't control myself."

———————

Throughout July, Joe encouraged me to explore my anger. Over time, I started to enjoy talking about one of Tom's mean comments so I could rant and rave about how awful my soon-to-be ex-husband was.

"Anger is energizing," Joe said. "Sadness is depleting."

"I can see that now. Here is what I don't get. When Tom didn't want me to express my anger, I went along with it. Many other women wouldn't have accepted living with a man who refused to speak to them when they were mad. I did, and I am not sure why."

"Let's go back further in your life," Joe said. "Tell me about a time when you were angry when you were young."

It took me a few seconds to figure out where to start. "I was an only child until I was eight, and my sister was born. When I was ten, and she was two, I was supposed to help get her dressed, but she wouldn't cooperate."

I remembered her hair swirling around her head as she launched herself from her bedroom mattress into the air like a trampoline artist in the circus. She refused to stay still. "Then I grabbed her and pushed her arm into the shirt she was struggling not to wear.

She started to cry. My mother came into the bedroom and yelled at me for hurting her."

As I described the situation to Joe, my face felt as if it had gone from pink to a burning red. I was talking about part of myself I always kept hidden.

"You know," Joe said. "Kids don't have much control over their anger, and that's the kind of stuff siblings always do when they're mad."

My shoulders relaxed. I had spent my entire life thinking something was wrong with how I expressed anger. According to Joe, however, my feeling was more normal than I realized.

"A parent's job is to help children learn to express their anger with words, rather than through physical aggression," he said.

"My mother had a short fuse and was a yeller. It would have never occurred to her to teach me a constructive way to handle anger because she didn't know how to do it herself," I said. "When I was young, I was scared of her."

"Maybe you didn't get mad at Tom because you didn't want to be like your mother," Joe said.

I paused. My eyes shifted to Joe, over to his window and back to him again. I imagined the soft, snapping sound the pieces of a jigsaw puzzle made when they fit together.

———

Two weeks later, I drove to my parents' New York home, my first visit since Tom had left. I arrived at dinner and after our meal, we carried our bowls of coffee ice cream to our usual spots in the family room. My father sat on the sofa, slipped off his shoes, and rested his feet on the coffee table. My mother settled into the recliner. I reclaimed the cozy corner of their white, nubby

L-shaped sofa, covering my feet with the blue and green afghan my mother had crocheted. At age eighteen, I had been eager to move out of their house and start my own life; as a thirty-two-year-old whose marriage had fallen apart, I was happy to be back in my comforting childhood home.

For much of the night, I talked non-stop about my marriage to Tom and my divorce. My parents had heard it all before but listened to me without any complaints. When I was done, I went to bed, hoping the safety of my parents' house would translate into a good night's sleep. I couldn't fall asleep here either. So finally, I put on my bathrobe and wandered into my dad's study, as I had often done before, looking for a new book.

I stood in front of a bookshelf that took up an entire wall. On the third shelf from the bottom, I saw a book called *Feelings* by Willard Gaylin. I wouldn't have picked it up if Joe and I hadn't spent the previous few weeks talking about anger. Now I was curious to see what this author had to say. So, I sat at my father's desk and scanned the table of contents.

Each chapter was devoted to a different emotion: anxiety, guilt, and shame, among others. There was even an entire chapter about the feeling of being used, which I had often felt since Tom's departure. I turned to the first chapter called "Feeling Free to Feel." Gaylin wrote that it is more important for people to acknowledge their feelings than to ask themselves whether they have a valid reason for having them.

I remembered my journal entries from the previous week. On Monday, I had written it was ridiculous I was still not over Tom. On Wednesday, I had berated myself for feeling hurt when my friend Patty told me she was too busy to have dinner with me.

Why was I over-sensitive, always making a mountain out of a molehill? Other people weren't upset when their friend was busy. Why couldn't I handle adversity like an adult?

Gaylin's book made me see that whenever I experienced a negative emotion, I questioned whether I was justified or over-reacting. No wonder I usually discounted my feelings. I flipped through several more pages. According to Gaylin, feelings were vital because they directed human behavior. For instance, fear warned us to avoid potential danger; pleasure led us towards a joyful event. Without emotions, there would be no way to understand what was safe and unsafe in the world. I thought about the implications of Gaylin's point of view. Every time I dismissed my distress as overreacting or being too sensitive, I didn't bother to identify what was causing my feelings in the first place.

When I returned for therapy the following week, I told Joe I had second-guessed so many emotions that I never noticed what was wrong in my marriage. "It was as if you had disconnected the radar system alerting you to an approaching danger," he said. He paused and shifted in his seat. Later, I would try to guess how long he had waited to pose the question on his mind. "Do you think Tom had someone else?" he asked.

My first reaction was to shake my head. The thought he was seeing someone else never even crossed my mind. Then I remembered his story about the department secretary who cried to him about her boyfriend. Perhaps he had been involved with her.

"If he was giving off cues, I didn't know how to pick them up," I said.

Years later, after practicing for a while, I realized almost all of my patients who abruptly left their spouses had someone waiting in the wings for them. The extra-marital affair often lasted only long enough to give the unfaithful partner the courage they needed to leave their marriage.

"I knew so little about Tom," I said to Joe. "Anything was possible."

CHAPTER 15

LISA

Two weeks after Christmas, Lisa was thinking of consulting a divorce attorney. She suspected Greg had already spoken to a lawyer; he liked to have the upper hand in situations where he might lose money. A friend gave Lisa the name of an attorney she had used saying, "This lawyer is a shark."

Lisa thought about making the call all week long. Yet every time she picked up her phone, she put it down again. When I asked her during one of our sessions whether she had contacted the attorney, she looked out the window, down at the floor, and finally back at me. She shook her head, slumping against the chair.

"What do you think is going on for you?" I asked.

The expression on her face shifted from discouraged to frustrated. "I wanted Greg to file," she said. "It's his fault we are getting a divorce. He should take responsibility for being the one to end the marriage." Her voice had a sharp, angry edge I rarely heard from her. I pictured steam coming out of her ears.

I blinked as a memory of my divorce came back to me. Thirty years ago, I had sat on one side of a highly polished, large oak desk, my attorney on the other. She had recommended I go along with Tom's request for a "no-fault" divorce. "It's better that way," she said, in a calm voice that hinted at how much more complicated and expensive this process would be if I contested the divorce. I turned my face away from hers, and my head bobbed up and down in a quiet, polite nod. Inside I was silently screaming: MY HUSBAND WANTS THIS DIVORCE, NOT ME. IT'S HIS FAULT. Then, just when I thought our meeting had reached its lowest point, I heard my lawyer say, "Tom told his attorney the divorce was your idea."

"What do you mean?" I asked.

She repeated what she had said: Tom had told his attorney the divorce was entirely my decision. He was filing to get over the inevitable.

"That's not true," I said.

"I know."

If Tom had been so ashamed of himself that he couldn't admit the truth, he had found the perfect solution. He would file for divorce and then tell people I was the person responsible for ending the marriage. My head felt like it was going to explode, but I had to agree to a "no-fault" divorce.

I walked out of the lawyer's office, drove to my apartment, and dove back into *Crazy Time*. What did the author have to say about the decision to divorce? As she explained it, the person who initiated the divorce becomes the "divorce seeker" and the other spouse becomes the "divorce opposer." The complicated and painful marital history bringing two people to the end of their marriage disappeared. It didn't matter who was the alcoholic, the spendthrift, or the screamer. One spouse took on the responsibility for initiating a divorce. The other spouse got to appear blameless, at least to the outside world: that was who Tom wanted to be.

————————

Lisa's loud cough interrupted my train of thought. "Why won't Greg file for a divorce already? My kids tell me he spends all his free time with the woman he has been having an affair with. Doesn't he want to get on with his new life with his girlfriend?"

I was as baffled as she was. Was Greg trying to keep Lisa wound around his little finger while he checked out his legal options? Or did he want to test out the new relationship with his girlfriend before he decided to get a divorce? I saw the direction of my thinking: suspicious and cynical about a man's intentions. I knew my troubled marriage to Tom lingered in the back of my mind, and I didn't want it to affect my work with Lisa. "Who knows why Greg won't go ahead with the divorce," I said. "You need to decide what *you* will do."

Lisa looked confused. Maybe she was trying to figure out how long she would have to wait for Greg to do something. Neither of them wanted to look like the person who wanted the divorce. They were in a stalemate. If I had to put money on it, I could guess who would break first. The statistics gave the story away. Many more women than men filed for divorce, and the gender difference was, in fact, wide: women initiated sixty-nine percent of all divorces. Experts have suggested men avoid filing for divorce because they have much to lose financially in court. I knew Greg's salary far outstripped Lisa's. Perhaps he believed the court would award Lisa less alimony if it looked like she was the party who wanted the divorce.

———————

By late March, Lisa had put off contacting an attorney for three months. Earlier in my career, I might have become impatient with her, urging her to make a decision she was not ready to make. I wanted patients to get better quickly because it made me feel like I was doing a good job. Now I know they set the pace, not me.

"I wonder why it is so hard for you," I asked.

"Every time I am on the verge of making a decision, I start to get frightened," she said. She scooched forward to the end of the chair.

"About what?"

"I don't know how to take care of our house as Greg does. I don't have a clue who I should call if something goes wrong," she said in a shaky voice. Lisa was worried about money, too. Greg took charge of their financial planning. He was a savvy business-man, or at least he cultivated that image. "I don't know anything about investments," she said. "I don't even know which bank our accounts are in." Lisa paused and shook her head. "I felt like we made a bargain when we got married. Greg promised to take care of me so I wouldn't have to do things I didn't have the confidence to try."

"What about all of your accomplishments?" I asked. "The kids, your job, keeping the house."

"I just did what was expected of me," she said.

Neither of us said anything for a few seconds. As she stared out the window, I thought about how similar she was to the younger version of myself. When Tom and I lived together decades earlier, I expected him to take care of the household chores I didn't know how to do, from unclogging the bathroom drain to haggling with a mechanic over the car repairs. The unspoken—and unexamined—bargain I made with Tom was the same one Lisa had made with Greg. I could avoid trying to do things I didn't know how to do, trusting Tom would take care of those tasks. Ultimately, when he left me, I was panic-stricken about having to manage my life alone.

Decades have passed since I was that fearful young woman. When I conjured her up in my mind, I was struck by all the accomplishments she cast aside to conclude she couldn't take care of herself. What about the PhD? And the papers at professional conferences? Didn't those achievements count for anything? I imagined grabbing the younger version of myself by my shoulders. *You had so many wonderful qualities*, I would say. *Why did you short-change yourself?*

———

Throughout the winter I saw Lisa, I was also treating a woman named Katrina. With her long hair and trendy jeans ripped at the knees, she fit the image of the sales manager of a vintage clothing boutique that she was. She came to see me because she feared she might lose her job.

During the first few months of treatment, Katrina spent many hours describing all the mistakes she believed she made at work. She was too quiet at meetings, making her colleagues think she had nothing to contribute. When she did speak, she stumbled over her words. Her hands shook. She was sure her boss thought she didn't know what she was talking about. Nevertheless, Katrina didn't lose her job. Her boss gave her a stellar performance review, followed by a promotion. "It was a fluke," she said. "Just good luck." Then she launched into another description of her professional errors.

The similarities between Katrina and Lisa were obvious. Both women emphasized their flaws, not their strengths. Lisa focused on the household chores she didn't know how to do; Katrina talked about her professional failings. I could see the younger version of myself reflected in both women.

The parallels between us made me consider why so many women lacked self-confidence. In *The Confidence Code*, Katy Kay and Claire Shipman, both highly accomplished women who realized they often downplayed their successes in life, addressed this question. They described the many women who similarly highlighted their deficiencies and ignored their achievements. Kay and Shipman presented various reasons why women struggled with a lack of self-confidence. First, there was a possible biological explanation. Brain imaging studies showed women created strong, long-lasting memories of adverse life events that caused them to think and rethink their mistakes. Consequently, their flaws, rather than their accomplishments, stood out for them. A second explanation underscored the role learning might play in women's lack of self-confidence. Parents and teachers didn't encourage girls to take risks and make mistakes as they did with boys. Facing challenges, failing, and picking yourself up again builds an individual's self-confidence. Yet young women didn't typically have this experience, again making it difficult for them to develop a belief in their abilities.

———

When I saw Lisa in April, she was so frustrated with herself for not yet contacting an attorney that I set aside my idea about sharing the research on female self-confidence and went back to helping her understand her reluctance to file for divorce.

"I just can't make a decision," she said. "I think about what I should do all the time. I'm caught in limbo. It's driving me crazy."

"There is only one way out," I said. "At some point, you will need to decide what to do." I used my gentle therapist voice, hoping I didn't sound too harsh. But I wanted to bring home the point that she was the only person who could get herself out of limbo.

We had been around the attorney issue so many times in the previous few months that I had lost count. I didn't know if her impasse was due to a lack of self-confidence or an entirely different issue. Of course, I kept my confusion to myself. The truth was, however, as much as I wanted Lisa to make a decision, I wasn't sure how to help her get there.

CHAPTER 16

ELLEN

My sweaty t-shirt stuck to my back as I bent over an open suitcase piled high with clothes in the bedroom of my new home. It was mid-September, and the still hot, late summer day had sucked out all my energy. Since Tom had left five months earlier, I'd retained a divorce attorney, packed up our apartment, and rented a U-Haul truck. Then I'd lugged my clothes, books, bureau, and desk into this tiny bedroom of a large, Victorian home in Boston. I shared the house with five roommates: a couple who owned the home, Wendy and Lou, and three men, all of us professional people in our thirties and forties.

I stood over my suitcase and surveyed my new room. The ten boxes of books I had brought would have to remain unpacked and pushed up against one of the walls; there was space for only one bookshelf. The foam mattress lay on top of the hardwood floor in the corner opposite me. *Get a frame and a box spring*, I said to myself. But I was tired. Too tired to do anything other than rub a tender spot on my lower back. Finally, I picked five blouses out of my suitcase. As I rotated around the room looking for a place to hang them, I realized my new bedroom lacked a closet. I sunk onto the floor and wiped the sweat off my forehead.

"At some point, you will go from sad to angry," Joe had reminded me, off and on all summer. He was right. When I thought about Tom, a tightness started in my jaw and crawled down my arms until it reached my hands which I balled into two tight fists. Sometimes, I imagined bashing the windshield of Tom's new Honda Civic, his pride and joy, with a baseball bat. Other times, I fantasized about the dull thud the bat might make if I cracked it against his skull.

———

By October, bright blue skies and cool breezes had replaced the humidity of Boston's summer. I rifled through one of the boxes in my bedroom and dug out my lecture notes on the Industrial Revolution. I placed my small, portable typewriter next to my notes. I glanced at it several times, and my shoulders sagged. The typewriter reminded me of the fifty tenure track teaching jobs I had applied for over the previous two years: all those applications and only one interview at the University of Southern Mississippi in Hattiesburg, a place I couldn't imagine calling home. They rejected me anyway.

Throughout the previous month I had driven back and forth to my teaching job at Boston College, worrying about my future. This was the second year of my "terminal" two-year contract, and I knew I should start looking for another job for the following year. Yet every night after work, I lay on my mattress and stared at the typewriter, trying to force myself to sit at the desk and bang out more cover letters. Why bother? I no longer believed I would get a permanent teaching position, and now, decades later,

I'm surprised it took me so long to reach that conclusion. There had been plenty of warnings. The look in my advisor's eyes when she told me I was a "good, not a great" student should have been enough. She appeared to be trying to telegraph a coded message to me. Get. Out. Now. Because, as it turned out, good historians were not good enough to find a job.

Just as I had done in my marriage, I overlooked the red flags, believing I could control the course of my life through sheer determination alone. I worked hard. Other people landed jobs, why not me? Unfortunately, an economic shift had taken place which I had ignored: too many PhD students for too few jobs. I didn't have as much control over my employment situation as I expected and needed a new career.

Over the next few days, I ran through several options. I thought of teaching history in high school, but my mother's frustrating stories about her experience as a high school teacher had already soured me on the thought. What about a corporate trainer in a bank? I once worked as a bank teller. Certainly, there were far worse jobs. Yet when I imagined teaching bank tellers how to handle demanding customers, I could see myself trying to stifle a wide yawn.

Late one night, unable to sleep, I wandered into the kitchen and plopped down at the table where one of my roommates, Lou, was having his midnight snack. He was a short, soft-spoken man, a professional social worker who often listened to me complain about my dead-end career on many of my worst days. "What else did you think about doing in your life?" he asked me, in such a quiet voice I had to lean forward to hear him.

I explained I had considered becoming a psychotherapist when I was in college. Since my grades weren't high enough to get into a graduate program, I gave up on the idea.

Lou spooned some ice cream into his mouth and told me the profession had changed. "The demand for psychotherapists has exploded over the past ten years," he said, "and new professional programs have opened up that accept lots of students."

I nodded at him and stood up to pull out some ice cream for myself. "One of those, the Massachusetts School of Professional Psychology, is only ten miles from here," Lou said.

My hand froze on the freezer door. I spun around and studied his moving lips. Despite his quiet voice, I had an image of him holding a megaphone and yelling the phrases "accepts lots of students" and then "only ten miles from here" right in my face.

I walked back to my bedroom, too keyed up to sleep. Despite my early aspirations, I hadn't thought about becoming a therapist at this stage of my life. Why not? I had been an undergraduate psychology major. The students in the history classes I taught often commented on the accepting attitude I created for them in the classroom. There was my own experience as a therapy patient as well. Joe had been an excellent mentor. By now, I could anticipate the questions he would ask me and the interpretations he would offer. Perhaps my treatment had turned into an unexpected apprenticeship.

The next morning I called the school for an application. It arrived two days later, but I felt too nervous to fill it out. I folded it back into tight thirds, slid it into its envelope, and left it on my desk. Two weeks later, I tried again. This time I shoved the application under a stack of library books. I was paralyzed. My gut told me to go to graduate school and become a psychotherapist, yet my brain pulled me in the opposite direction. It made me reluctant to heed my gut, reminding me of my many mistakes. I didn't trust myself to make a good decision.

The following Tuesday, I was back on Joe's sofa, listening to the familiar hum of his white noise machine. "I think I want to become a psychotherapist, but I can't decide," I said.

"Why not?" Joe asked.

"I have different scenarios going through my head," I said. "All of them have a bad ending."

"Do you ever think about the possible positive outcomes?"

"Sometimes," I said. "Then I get bombarded by my disaster fantasies. It could take the entire session to describe all of them."

"Pick the important ones."

"What would happen if after four years of graduate school, I disliked being a therapist?

"Go out and look for a different job," Joe said.

"Yes, but it would be humiliating to start over again."

Then there were my concerns about money. My parents had paid for college, so I wasn't saddled with debt. This time I would have to take out a large student loan to pay the thousands of dollars in tuition.

"You aren't in debt right now," Joe said. "Why wouldn't you be able to find a way to pay back a loan?"

"You have more confidence in me than I have in myself," I said, as a creeping deflated feeling threatened to overtake me. "There is one more fear. This one seems like a carryover from adolescence. I won't fit into the graduate program. Maybe all the other students will be fresh out of college. They'll think I'm too old to be their friend."

Both of us were quiet. "That's it," I said. "Those are the big worries."

"Why do you think you can't stop worrying?" Joe asked.

My fears had so consumed me I didn't know how to answer the question. I had never tried to step back and figure it out. It took me a few seconds to find the right words. "When I married Tom, I knew, in theory, my marriage might not work out. One of my cousins had gotten divorced earlier. Twice, in fact. I thought I wouldn't end up like her because I had made a careful, smart choice of a husband."

I watched Joe nod, embarrassed by how naive my twenty-four-year-old self had been.

"The same was true for my career. As soon as I started graduate school in history, I heard students who were almost done with their degrees talking about how few teaching positions there were. I never imagined I would be one of those people who wouldn't get a job. I assumed I would be the exception. Why in the world did I think I was so special?"

"Now what?" Joe asked.

"Tom leaving me and not getting a teaching job has shown me my life choices can turn into a mess. Knowing that makes me afraid to make another important decision, which might also prove to be a mistake."

Neither of us said anything. Joe placed his elbows on his knee, as I had seen him do many times before when he was about to say something he really wanted me to think about. "The challenge is to find a way to go forward in life, even though you know it might not turn out the way you want it. It requires courage, I guess, and also an awareness that if your decision turns out to be a mistake, you can always make another decision to correct it."

"Oh," I said to Joe, hoping he would give me detailed instructions about how to do this.

"Let's say you go back to school, and you decide being a therapist is not what you want to do," he said. "You can leave the program. I know the financial situation would be complicated, but it is not impossible. Think of it this way, a decision is the first step, not the final one."

I remained quiet, glancing out of the window. I had never thought about a decision that way. Before, it seemed like something I was supposed to get "right" after careful consideration. I liked the idea that a choice was a beginning move. I could change my mind if I needed to. If I looked at a decision from this perspective, it seemed less risky.

At home that evening, I went over the therapy session again. I knew I wanted a fresh beginning and returning to school seemed the best way to get one. The fear of messing up my life hadn't gone away, however. It was a feeling I would have to learn to tolerate. Joe was right. I could always go down a different path if the school didn't work out. I would keep getting better and better at starting over.

A few days later, I slid the completed application into the mailbox. Then, in January, I received a telephone call inviting me to an interview. Two weeks later, I donned the outfit I had worn to my interview at the University of Southern Mississippi—tweedy, cranberry-colored suit, blue silk blouse, and low black heels—and drove to the Massachusetts School of Professional Psychology,

MSPP as it was called at the time. A secretary showed me to the waiting area where I sat, trying to ignore the knot in my gut.

The admissions director walked toward me, shook my hand, and showed me into her office. Her first question was why I wanted to make a career change. Of course, there was no way I could avoid the topics of my divorce and aborted career in history, although by now, at least, I could give an abbreviated version without crying. She leaned back in her chair, listening with the same level of concentration I had noticed in Joe. So that was what it was like to be interviewed by a psychotherapist. "Lots of our students are older and are going through transitions in their lives," she said.

In the months since Tom had left, I spent many hours thinking about my losses; marriage, children, and career had vanished. My interview made me think differently about my life. I imagined myself like a molting animal, shedding its outer layer of skin to grow larger. Going back to school gave me a chance to start all over again, just as I wanted.

I drove home from the interview, wishing the next few months would fly by so the April deadline would arrive and I could find out if I had been accepted into the graduate program. But, within the week, my mind had shifted to a different deadline—March 25, the court date for my divorce. My stomach tightened as I thought about seeing Tom again, the first time in ten months. Would he look at me? Would he say anything? What would I say to him?

I dressed carefully that early spring morning, buttoning and unbuttoning the jacket of my cranberry suit several times before I walked out the door. My friend, Cara, had agreed to come with me, and I picked her up on the way to the courthouse. I was so nervous I bolted for the ladies' room as soon as I walked inside, leaning against the cold metal stall sick with anxiety. Cara rapped on the stall door. "It's time to go," she said.

We walked into the courtroom together. From the corner of my eye, I saw Tom dressed in a dark business suit, a white shirt, and a red tie. At first, I mistook him for a lawyer.

"All rise," announced the court official. The judge entered the room. He called each of us up to the bench. I agreed to the divorce conditions, as my husband did: seven years of marriage severed in five minutes.

For ten months I had been rehearsing the speeches I wanted to deliver to Tom, long sermons about his disloyalty, a lecture about his cowardice in blindsiding me, and accusations about another woman. I knew this would be my only chance. Before I could say anything, my now ex-husband turned his back on me, as he had done so many times when we were still married, and began walking toward the courtroom exit. I opened my mouth but couldn't remember the words I intended to say. Suddenly, I became a ten-year-old girl again, flinging out the only angry word I could think of.

"Turd," I hissed at the back of his head as he walked out the door.

Cara grabbed my arm and led me away.

In the drive to the courtroom earlier that morning, I had told Cara I expected to end up in Joe's office for an emergency appointment after seeing Tom in court. Instead, she had another plan in mind. "What about the Ritz Hotel for brunch," she asked. "Go see your therapist later."

By 11 am, we sat in the Ritz, stirring our Bloody Marys with a celery stalk. The sharp bite of Tabasco sauce hit the back of my tongue. "Do you think Tom heard what I said to him?" I asked. "At least I had the last word."

Cara shrugged her shoulders. "Tom doesn't matter anymore," she said. "You're divorced. Whatever happens next in your life is up to you. This is your chance to bounce back." She picked up her glass. When she clinked mine, it made the sound of a clear, bright piano note.

Two weeks later, I walked in from work and headed for the kitchen table where one of my roommates had deposited the mail. I saw the long, white envelope, thick and heavy, just the way my college acceptance letter had been. I ripped it open and read those first few words, "We are pleased to inform you ..." A grin overtook my face. Lou was standing at the sink, washing dishes. When he turned around, I smiled at him. He slapped my hand in a high five. Cara was right. Whatever happened next was up to me.

CHAPTER 17

ELLEN

The MSPP orientation meeting was scheduled for an evening in mid-August, a few weeks before the start of school. Early in the afternoon, I planned my outfit. I decided to ditch the cranberry tweed suit I had worn on previous important occasions: unsuccessful job interviews, my divorce hearing. I was starting my life over, and I didn't need any reminders of my painful past. I wanted to think of myself as a student again, not a professor. Beige slacks and a bright turquoise blouse seemed just right. A new look, relaxed but professional.

On my drive to the meeting my stomach felt like a gymnast practicing somersaults. Now, thanks to eighteen months of psychotherapy, I understood the source of feelings like this. These were old fears about whether I would make friends. My shy nature, rejection experienced in middle and high school, and lack of dating success before Tom had diminished my confidence in social situations. Insight, however, hadn't removed the fear, and I wondered if anyone would talk to me at the orientation meeting. I calmed myself down with a trick I had learned in therapy. I reminded myself my discomfort would disappear when I started talking to someone, a piece of advice Joe gave me that I would share with many of my therapy patients over the next thirty years.

On top of this, a new worry was bubbling under the surface. All the incoming students were expected to begin seeing psychotherapy patients a month after school started. An experienced psychotherapist would be supervising my work, meeting with me twice weekly to discuss the cases. How would I know what to do? When I thought about how much I had discovered about the power of empathy from Joe, however, I calmed down a little; at the least, I could draw upon this skill as a novice therapist.

I sat down in the MSPP auditorium. The dean introduced himself. He described the program, and his message was reassuring: the school's goal was to create a supportive environment for students to learn how to be therapists. There would be a nurturing quality, just like in therapy itself, I realized. Training to become a psychotherapist sounded like it was going to be different from anything I had encountered in the many years I had spent in various higher education institutions.

The dean announced we would take a break for wine and cheese. I picked up a glass of white wine and surveyed my classmates. There were twenty-five women and eight men. Half of them appeared my age or older. Before I could walk away with my wine, the woman behind me in line asked me where I was from.

"Boston," I said. "How about you?"

"Colorado."

She had owned a small antique shop in Boulder and decided she wanted a change. Part of my brain was listening to the story, and another part was jumping up and down with joy that the first person I spoke to was beginning her life over again, just like me. It looked like MSPP would be a better place to start a new chapter of life than I could have ever imagined.

The dean called us back for a few closing remarks. I took a deep breath and smelled the familiar musty chalk dust odor permeating the air. I sat back and relaxed, opened my notebook and smoothed out the clean white page. I knew how to be a student, even if I didn't know how to become a psychotherapist. I felt like I had come home after a long difficult journey.

––––––––––

On a Tuesday evening two weeks later, I slung my canvas book bag filled with school supplies over my shoulder and arrived on time for my first class, Lifespan Development. The teacher, Bob Kegan, had pushed the desks into a circle so all thirty-five students would be arranged around him. He explained the course would cover psychological development from infancy to adulthood.

As he went through the syllabus, Kegan spoke in long, dense, complicated sentences. Occasionally, he took a quick breath and dove right back into his topic. I scribbled fast, trying to get it all down. He repeated the words "adult development," and I underlined them in my notebook each time. Since my divorce, I had changed so much I hardly felt like the same person I was during my marriage. Perhaps my Lifespan Development class would provide insight into how this transformation occurred. I imagined Kegan's gaze narrowing into a laser beam pointed right in my direction, as if his lecture was just for me.

––––––––––

Tuesdays were Kegan. Thursdays were a class called Integrative. In this course, we would apply Kegan's lifespan development theory to the patients we would soon be treating. The MSPP philosophy was that psychotherapists needed to understand themselves, before they took care of other people. Consequently, our Integrative instructor explained we would also look at our personal histories through the lens of lifespan development theory.

"Let's start by getting to know each other," she said.

I shifted in my seat, trying to get comfortable. I couldn't decide if I should volunteer to go first to get it over with or go last, hoping we would run out of time before I had a chance to speak. The instructor took the decision out of my hands. She asked the man sitting to my right to begin.

In a voice barely above a whisper, he told the class about the loss of both of his parents in a plane crash when he was a little boy. We were all quiet. A woman on the other side of him gently patted his hand. Then another classmate took her turn. She laughed and cried through a description of the shoplifting obsession she developed at ten years old, when her dad was dying of cancer. "I think I wanted someone just to notice me," she said, as her voice cracked.

When my turn came, I described my divorce, tearing up in a way I hadn't done for many months. The instructor handed me a tissue box. A classmate across the room smiled at me. Despite the hard surface of the chair, I felt as comfortable here as I did on Joe's sofa. The training to be a therapist seemed similar to therapy itself: empathy was central to both.

By October, I could see it would be impossible not to make friends. Personal conversations that began in class spilled into the hallway or continued as we gathered on the lawn outside the school on those warm, Indian summer days. I made friends with four other women around my age who were also divorced, and we took turns cooking dinner for each other on Friday nights. My worries about not fitting in evaporated.

———————

A few weeks later, I had to confront my second fear about school: treating psychotherapy patients. My placement was at a community mental health center south of Boston. During our first meeting, my clinical supervisor, Chuck, filled me in on the patient, Maria, I would be seeing. She was a thirty-nine-year-old married woman struggling with depression after two miscarriages. At this point, Maria was worried she wouldn't get pregnant again because of her age, and if she did, she wouldn't be able to carry a baby to term.

I was nervous before the session, but I was looking forward to it, too. While I didn't know how to do therapy, I knew what it was like to want a baby and not have one. I hoped I would communicate a sense of understanding that would create an initial bond between us.

Nothing went the way I planned. In our first meeting I told her I was a student and would be closely supervised by an experienced therapist. She frowned, disappointed, or so it seemed, to have a student trainee as her therapist. How could I fault her? I would have felt the same way.

The treatment went downhill from there. We met weekly for the next month. She was a quiet woman who gave one- or two-word answers to my questions. No matter how empathic I tried to be, nothing I said seemed to resonate with her. Then, after a month of therapy, she didn't show up for her scheduled appointment.

"What did I do wrong?" I asked my supervisor during our weekly meeting, expecting he would dissect my poor skills.

Instead, he asked a question that surprised me: how did talking to this patient make me feel? "Therapists can use their emotional reactions to a patient as data to understand the person better," he said.

"What do you mean?"

"Let's say you are talking to a patient and feeling bored. You might want to ask yourself if the patient is talking in a monotone because she is afraid of her feelings."

I thought about the few sessions I had had with Maria. I felt disengaged from her, as if nothing I could do would please her. I kept working harder to find the right thing to say. When that didn't work, I began to feel helpless. Helplessness soon shifted into a feeling of irritation.

"If I am going to be completely honest, I was relieved she didn't come back," I said. "I didn't like feeling helpless."

I felt uneasy, as if I had blurted out something I shouldn't have said. But supervision felt so similar to a psychotherapy session, it felt okay to be honest.

"What do you think that was about?" Chuck asked, as if he were channeling my therapist, Joe.

I glanced at the clock, the door, and the office window. There was no escape. I would have to have a very personal discussion about my marriage and divorce with someone I barely knew. I described the abrupt end to my marriage when Tom decided he didn't want a child. Despite my efforts not to cry, my eyes watered up. Chuck nudged the tissue box toward me. "Maybe your experience is affecting how you interacted with this patient more than you realized," he said in a soft voice designed to instruct me on how to be an effective therapist without making me feel embarrassed about my divorce or damaging my fragile self-esteem.

He was right. My desire for a child had often played in the background of my mind since school had started. I just had to think back to my Integrative class the previous week. We were discussing babies, and one of the students brought her son in for a real-life demonstration of toddlers. All ten of us sat in a circle, watching the baby wobble back and forth as we waited to see if the fourteen-month-old would leave his mom and make it to his teddy bear on the chair three feet away. No one said a word. Finally, the mother pried her son's hand out of hers. He took two tentative steps, leaned forward, and then teetered backward. Down he went, his cushioned bottom making a muffled plop when he hit the floor.

"Uh oh," his mom laughed.

As the teacher and my classmates discussed secure attachment in babies, I gripped the smooth surface of the ballpoint pen and tried to concentrate on taking notes. I felt so sad. Each time I glanced at the baby, I longed for one of my own.

This wasn't the first event to rekindle my yearning for an infant. I had felt the same way during a phone conversation with an old college friend a few days earlier. Rebecca and I had been out of touch for two years. She called around 8 pm one night, telling me a mutual friend had told her about my divorce. I filled her in on the details as she made sympathetic noises on the other end of the line. Finally, she said she had something to tell me.

"What?" I asked.

"I wanted to tell you I got divorced, too."

I was shocked. From the outside, she appeared to have a perfect life. Then she discovered her husband had been having an affair with a co-worker for years. One day he announced he wanted to marry this other woman. He and Rebecca divorced, and he and his new wife had twin girls the following year. "I'm thirty-three," Rebecca said. "The worst thing is that I doubt I will ever have a baby."

The crack of pain in her voice came across clearly through the telephone connection. I heard her blow her nose, and I wondered why she was giving up on her dream of a family. She was young enough to meet a new man. Or, she could even have a child or adopt one on her own. The feminist movement had made it more acceptable to become a mother without a partner, and I was beginning to think about this route for myself.

In that afternoon supervision meeting with Chuck, I confessed a thought I had about my patient, Maria. At least she had a partner to try to have a baby with. That was more than I had.

"How do you think this affected your work with her?" he asked.

"Perhaps it made me less understanding of her than I could have been. Maybe she picked up on my jealousy."

"Keep this idea in mind next time you see a patient whose experience reminds you of your own," Chuck said.

———

I was relieved when my Lifespan Development and Integrative classes finished discussing infants, toddlers, and young children; the classroom reminders exacerbated my sense of loss. Adolescence was our next topic.

According to Kegan, teenagers were in the interpersonal or socialized level of development. Unlike youngsters who looked at the world in terms of their own needs, teens could put themselves in another person's shoes and imagine a point of view different from their own. This awareness was a double-edged sword. On the one hand, teenagers understood and internalized social norms, making them more mature and reliable than younger children. On the other hand, the interpersonal pull was so strong that adolescents often made decisions based on what others in their life thought they should do, rather than thinking independently and deciding on their own.

Kegan said some people remained in the interpersonal stage of development well into their adult years. Others moved on to the next level, the self-authored stage of development. In this phase, people no longer shaped their lives according to social norms and expectations. While they understood what their spouse or neighbors might expect of them, they made independent decisions on their own behalf, even if their choice conflicted with these expectations.

Every day in the Lifespan Development course, I felt as if my brain was going in two directions. Part of me was trying to understand the details of Kegan's thinking; another part was trying to figure out how my life matched his ideas. I was doing just what I was supposed to do: test Kegan's theory against my own life experiences. During the second semester, everything fell into place.

Kegan argued that people's "self" changed throughout their lives, depending on their developmental stage. I looked at my life through the lens of his thinking and could see what he was talking about. The self I was when I was married to Tom was still interpersonal and adolescent in many ways. Tom, my parents, and even my graduate school advisor all shaped how I thought of myself. I couldn't make a decision without considering what *they* thought was right or wrong. Even though I was married and in my early thirties, I remained stuck in the interpersonal phase. If it weren't for my divorce, I might have stayed there for my entire life.

Later, when I became a therapist, I realized how often patients, including Lisa and Meghan, remained trapped in the interpersonal stage, just as I had been. My goal for them became the same one I had adopted for myself. Don't get bogged down in other people's opinions about what you should do. Make decisions on your own. Work towards becoming a self-authored individual.

———————

As my first year of school was coming to a close in May, I had a psychotherapy appointment with Joe. I had seen less of him that year than the previous one. With four classes each week, books to read, and papers to write, I had switched to biweekly sessions. A sign of progress, we both agreed.

"How's everything?" he said as soon as I sat down.

"Good," I said. The classes felt safe. I had learned a lot about how to be a therapist. Most importantly, I was doing well, with excellent grades and outstanding evaluations from my teachers and clinical supervisor. The self-doubts I had about school were fading away.

I thought of the term "corrective emotional experience" that Chuck, my supervisor, had used one day when we discussed a case. A corrective emotional experience was how a supportive, caring therapist helped a patient have a different emotional reaction to a past challenging life event. School had been my corrective emotional experience, transforming how I looked at my history. Events that had previously appeared to be disastrous mistakes now seemed like lessons designed to teach me about how I wanted to live my life in the future. For example, my divorce, pushing me from the interpersonal stage to the self-authoring one, had changed from being the worst thing in my life to the best thing that ever happened to me. The evolution of a new life story was what healing was about, I could see now, as I was on my way to becoming a psychotherapist myself.

"School turned out to be a great decision," Joe said. He grinned as if he knew it would be a wise choice all along.

CHAPTER 18

MEGHAN

Around Halloween, Meghan interrupted her litany of complaints about Patrick with a surprising story. A few days earlier, her daughter had started crying at 2 am. Meghan was drifting in and out of sleep, buried under a soft, down comforter. She prayed her toddler would stop crying on her own and fall back to sleep. She felt her husband turn over on his side of the bed. Before she knew it, he jumped up to check on their daughter. "I didn't even have to ask him," Meghan said.

"That's good," I said, expecting to see a smile spread across her face, but it never came.

Two weeks later, she mentioned Patrick had done the laundry on Saturday morning. A happy fantasy of the two of them popped into my mind. I imagined Meghan waking up late in the morning, realizing her husband had gotten up with their daughter so she could sleep in. She could hear him in the kitchen playing with their little girl. She could burrow under the covers and listen to the deep, satisfying vibration of the washer's spin cycle. Music to her ears.

"Great," I said, expecting her to nod in agreement. But she kept her head perfectly still.

"I thought Patrick didn't help me because he didn't know what to do," she said. "Or he couldn't multitask like me. Now I see he was more capable than I realized all along." Her voice started and stopped in a kind of confusion I rarely heard from her. "How is it possible to live with someone for years and not know important things about them?" she asked.

"You would be surprised how often that happens," I said. My mind drifted back decades to my marriage. I had known so little about Tom, including the many years of built-up resentments he kept from me. Thirty years of listening to my patients, however, had made me see my ex-husband differently. Perhaps Tom had been too frightened to plumb the depth of his resentment because he would have had to acknowledge a desire to divorce me he didn't want to face. As I sat across from Meghan, I noticed I didn't feel my white-hot anger at my ex-husband any longer. Rage had been replaced by a gentler emotion, a feeling of understanding. I was beginning to forgive Tom.

"At least you were pleasantly surprised," I said. I waited for her to agree, but she didn't seem pleasantly surprised. She was still frowning.

Right after Thanksgiving, Meghan told me Patrick had given in to her desire for a second child.

"Why did he change his mind?" I asked.

"He realized how badly I wanted a sibling for our daughter."

I suspected Patrick also realized he was fighting a losing battle; unless the couple had another baby, Meghan would leave him. What would his acquiescence do to the future of their marriage in the long run? Would they reconcile now, only to have Patrick's resentment destroy the marriage later?

I looked at Meghan and wondered if Patrick stood a chance to get back in her good graces. The lines of frustration around her eyes remained as deeply etched as ever. If his offer to get up with their daughter in the middle of the night and his new-found enthusiasm for laundry hadn't done enough to soften Meghan, what about his willingness to have another kid? Would that transform her view of him? Or was it too little too late?

I had seen this pattern in patients many times before. Another couple, Stephanie and Bill, came to mind. They were in their late thirties, married for ten years, with two young boys. Stephanie's long dark hair gave her a dramatic flair, and Bill's neatly trimmed beard made him look like the computer scientist he was. Stephanie had always wanted more emotional closeness from her husband. He was too preoccupied with work to have the deep heart-to-heart talks she longed for. So the two co-existed with one another. Their conversations were limited to the chores of raising the kids and taking care of their house. When they came to see me, they were looking for their marriage to change. Stephanie acknowledged she had built a wall around herself, asking as little of Bill as possible. Bill said he understood he needed to be more open with his wife.

The couple could have stepped out of a book by my favorite marital therapist, John Gottman. According to therapist Terry Gaspard, Gottman found that by the time many couples came for therapy, they had endured six years of an unhappy marriage and resented each other so much that the marriage therapy was of little use. As Gottman would have predicted, three months of weekly sessions for Stephanie and Bill did not improve the marriage. She had become so emotionally distant from her husband that the love and attraction she once felt for him had disappeared. Bill felt almost like a stranger to her. Too little too late, I said to myself at the time. With Meghan sitting across from me in my office, the same thought came to my mind, and I suspected my job was to encourage her to explore a deep unhappiness in her marriage that she preferred to ignore.

————

Meghan showed up early for an appointment two weeks before Christmas. She hung her down parka on my coat rack, sunk into the comfy chair, and began telling me about a problematic student in her class. "He sits in the back of the room playing with his phone," she said, shaking her head back and forth. For the next twenty minutes Meghan reported on the challenges of a public school teacher, describing another difficult student and the vice-principal who had yet to call the student's parents to discuss the problem.

"Teaching has become a really frustrating profession," I said.

"Yes," she said. "Especially this time of year. The kids have a harder time concentrating right before Christmas vacation."

I studied her face, trying to gauge whether I should address the professional challenges she had brought up or bring her back to discussing her marriage. Before I could say anything, Meghan told me she wasn't excited about Christmas. She dreaded it.

I tried to picture her house on Christmas day: a tree decorated with red and green ornaments, twinkling white lights on the living room mantle. Her daughter would play with the silky ribbons, crinkly wrapping paper, and rough cardboard boxes. Meghan and

Patrick might be cordial to each other as they exchange gifts and avoid each other's gaze.

Meghan paused. She slumped against the back of the chair and knitted her fingers together into a tight ball. A few more seconds of silence stretched across the room. Her eyes flitted back and forth, from the door to the window and back again. Door, window, door, window.

I could tell she wanted to say something. I glanced at the clock. There were ten minutes left in the session. I'd been caught in this psychotherapeutic dilemma before. If I encouraged her to express her mind, I risked opening up a topic for discussion we wouldn't have the time to explore. It might leave her feeling worse, not better. Yet if I made the opposite choice—ignoring her need to get something off her chest—she could feel misunderstood. I hoped this wouldn't become a "doorknob moment," as therapists referred to it, where the patient stands up to leave, grabs hold of the doorknob, and reveals a deep secret right before she walks out.

Meghan was too much of a take-charge person to do that. She cleared her throat. "I know I should be excited about Christmas, but I'm not. I have been thinking about Patrick. Even with all the changes he has made, I'm not as happy as I thought I would be."

She blinked and looked out my office window. My eyes followed hers until we both stared at the deep blue December sky. She straightened out her jacket. Then she looked down at her skirt and rubbed at a piece of imaginary lint clinging to the fabric. Finally, Meghan looked right into my eyes. I watched her push her hair back. She plucked a tissue from the box on the table next to her, held on to the corner and dabbed it under her eyes.

"I don't think I am in love with Patrick anymore," Meghan said. "I am not sure I ever really loved him."

"That's painful to admit," I said. "It takes a lot of courage."

"I don't know what to do next," she said. "I'm afraid this will be the last Christmas the three of us will spend together as a family." Her eyes filled up. When she didn't look away or apologize for her tears, I realized she was becoming more comfortable with her feelings.

"People grieve when they think about ending a marriage, just as they do when their partner walks out on them," I said, handing her the tissue box. "Let's start here next time."

By January, the temperature in Meghan and Patrick's marriage mirrored the seemingly endless cold of New England in late winter. They tried to act as normal as they could around their daughter. Meghan told me it felt like they were roommates. Then, of course, there was the problem of sex. Meghan's interest in sex had disappeared along with her feelings for Patrick. Something had to change. On a Thursday afternoon, she came in and told me she had decided what to do.

"I think Patrick and I should separate. It doesn't have to be permanent, just a trial. It is so uncomfortable living with him like this," she said. "What do you think?"

I had treated some couples who benefited from an agreed period of separation. Jennifer and Mark had been married for twenty-five years when Jen discovered her husband had been unfaithful. Mark swore it had been a casual relationship. He and this woman had met in a bar and had sex in a hotel. He didn't have any feelings for her. Jennifer was hurt and angry, and every conversation between her and Mark turned into a bitter argument. "I know how I am reacting isn't helping us stay together. I don't feel like I can control myself right now," Jennifer said.

They needed some distance from one another to calm down and have productive conversations. When Jennifer suggested the two of them live apart for two months, I seconded her idea. Mark would live with his sister. He and Jen would talk on the phone every other day. Neither of them would date other people. They would come to see me for marital therapy each week. They both shared the goal of reconciling, not staying apart. At the end of the two months, I could see the separation had benefited them. It gave them a cooling-off period, helping them discuss the reasons for Mark's affair and Jennifer's feelings. After two months, Mark moved back home.

I wasn't sure about Meghan and Patrick. It was possible a separation might help them. However, I suspected Meghan was further along in her decision to split up permanently with Patrick than she admitted to herself.

"What do you think being separated is going to be like?" I said.

"I don't know," she said. "It is kind of a test to see if I miss my husband."

The next problem was who was going to live where. It made sense for Meghan to stay in the house since she did the lion's share of the childcare. Where would Patrick go? He didn't have any family nearby to live with, and he didn't want to ask friends if he could bunk down with them. Meghan had already figured out the details, with her characteristic thoroughness. Her parents were in North Carolina for the winter, and their Massachusetts condo stood empty. She and Patrick could take turns living there. "I'll go for half a week. Then Patrick can go for the other half," she told me. Meghan had arranged all the details of the separation from Patrick, just as she had cleaned his dorm room in college. I could see the parallels and hoped Meghan could see them, too.

The couple lived apart for two weeks. "It was great," Meghan told me when she returned for her next session. It was so peaceful at her parents' place. Even the days when she was with her daughter alone were calmer. The tension in the house was gone; she wasn't walking around trying to avoid Patrick.

There was also an unexpected benefit. She and Patrick communicated better. "When I told him I wished he would take more initiative, I think he really heard what I was saying. He thought it made sense to find activities to engage him, a new hobby or even a new job."

I had never heard her sound as enthusiastic about Patrick as she did at that moment.

"I told my girlfriend I might fall in love with my husband again. Or, maybe just for the first time," she said.

When Meghan left my office, I felt upbeat, too. Her joy at the thought of her marriage coming back to life was infectious, just as her hopelessness had been in an earlier session. I liked a fairy-tale happy ending to a story as much as anyone, particularly for patients like Meghan, to whom I felt so attached. Nevertheless, I warned myself not to jump the gun; my many years as a therapist taught me it took more than a quick separation to repair a marriage.

The day Meghan's daughter got sick everything changed. It turned out to be just a bad cold. Still, the little girl woke up crying every few hours for several nights running. Meghan took care of her daughter for the first two days and dragged herself to work each morning. On the third day, she put her head down on her desk and dozed off during her free period at school, waking up with a start when the bell for the kids to change classes clanged loudly. Finally, she called Patrick and asked him to come back for a couple of nights to help with their daughter.

I understood Meghan's exhaustion. It was the kind that makes a mother feel like she can't think straight, a brain as wobbly as jello. Maybe that was why she turned so quickly to Patrick for help. Nonetheless, I wished she had called someone other than her husband or, better yet, trudged through this difficult time alone. It would have given her a clearer sense of what it would be like to be a single mom, although I doubt it would have changed an outcome that was quickly becoming apparent to me.

Meghan thought Patrick would return to the condo after their daughter got well. He refused, and I wasn't sure I blamed him. Patrick wanted to try to solve their problems living together, not apart. Perhaps he assumed since he was doing his share of the household chores and had agreed to have a second child, she would be pleased with him. Meghan didn't see it that way. She tried to convince him they could solidify some of the positive steps they were taking if they had more time apart. I could see her point, too. But Patrick wouldn't budge. Whatever progress they had made quickly disappeared. Within two weeks, the couple had slipped back into their old patterns. Patrick avoided household chores. Meghan became irritated. Their brief separation hadn't improved anything; from Patrick's point of view, this option was off the table. The stakes were higher than they had ever been.

CHAPTER 19

Six weeks after Tom left, I went on my first date. A man I had met at a friend's wedding had scribbled my phone number on a cocktail napkin and asked me out for dinner a few days later. I felt elated and scared at the same time. I hadn't been on a date with a new man since I had met Tom ten years earlier. Yet, no matter how much trepidation I felt, I didn't consider declining his invitation. I wanted to see what dating would be like at this stage of my life. Plus, I imagined myself thumbing my nose at Tom, boasting about how quickly I had found someone who wanted to go out with me.

My date suggested an Italian restaurant, and I got decked out for the occasion: a short, swinging skirt, lavender blouse, and delicate sandals. We sat across from one another in a small red booth and scanned the menus. Over a plate piled high with pasta Bolognese, he told me about his law practice. He leaned forward as he talked, and I leaned away from him. His eyes locked onto mine as if they were drawn together by a magnetic force. My brain registered male interest. I kept my head steady for several seconds and stared back at him. Finally, I looked down at my plate of pasta, carefully twirling a slippery strand around my spoon. I squinted and glanced at his watch, calculating how many minutes until the date would end.

When I got home, I called my mom to describe the dinner. "I felt so uncomfortable," I said. "I'm not used to intense eye contact from a man I have just met. It was as if I had forgotten a custom from some foreign country. I don't want to go out with him again."

Six months later, I had a date with someone I met at a New Year's Eve party. He liked how I danced and called me several days later, inviting me to the movies. We went back to his apartment after the film. Recovering from a divorce meant having sex with someone other than Tom, and I accomplished my goal that night. According to *Crazy Time*, post-divorce sex could be exciting, but my night felt perfunctory and joyless. I felt more depressed than I had since those first few weeks after Tom left.

"Sex isn't going to make your grief go away," Joe said during my appointment after that date.

"I don't think I'm ready to go out with anyone right now," I said. The concerned look on Joe's face made me suspect he agreed with me.

———

It wasn't until the summer after my first year of graduate school—two years after Tom had left—I tried dating again. A classmate offered to introduce me to her boyfriend's old roommate who was in town for the weekend. "Go out to dinner with him. Maybe you'll like him," she said. "Just remember he is going back to San Francisco after the weekend."

I dressed in a sexy sundress, low cut with spaghetti straps. After a lobster dinner, two glasses of wine, and a conversation about a play we had both seen, we walked back to my apartment. The moonlight made his black hair glitter in the dark. Knowing he was going to leave town in forty-eight hours helped me let down my guard; I didn't have to worry about paying attention to any warning signs—the ones I had missed with Tom—because this man wasn't going to hang around long enough for me to pick them up. Also, I didn't have to contemplate whether or not we might have a future together because he was returning to California.

That night my body felt jazzed up in a way it hadn't for the previous two years of being single. It was as if a hidden passion switch suddenly flicked on. Twenty-four hours of bed, Chinese takeout, and a long, romantic walk around a pond the following day was more fun with a man than I had had in such a long time.

————

Throughout my second year in graduate school, I felt as if I was ready for a serious relationship. I couldn't find a man to date, however. My friends didn't know any eligible men with whom they could fix me up. My graduate school class was primarily women. There were bars, of course, but the idea of trying to carry on a conversation with a man in a room full of beer-breathed people turned my stomach.

I considered trying a dating service. With the increasing divorce rate, these services filled a niche by helping single people find each other. One television ad for the service called Together featured an attractive woman, "Joan," about my age, staring into the camera, describing her difficulty meeting anyone to go out with, and claiming the dating service had introduced her to the man of her dreams. Their fees, anywhere from $250 to $750, exceeded my current graduate school budget.

I started perusing the personal ad section of the *Boston Phoenix*, a local alternative newspaper. I usually picked up my free copy at Boston College, where I continued to teach history part-time. For a few weeks, I circled the ads that appealed to me and dumped the newspaper in the garbage. The sour whiff of desperation seemed to cling to personal ads. Didn't only losers resort to meeting people this way?

I thought about my options. I could continue doing nothing, hoping to lock eyes with a potential date at the grocery checkout line. Or, I could get over my attitude and take a chance on meeting someone through an ad. I chose the latter.

For much of my second year of school, I went out with men I met through the *Phoenix*, usually only once or twice. I quickly got the hang of the system. The man typically placed the ad. I wrote a letter in response, crafting it to let a potential date know I was divorced, in graduate school to become a psychotherapist, and, most importantly, looking for a serious relationship. I didn't include a photo, and no one expected one. If the man liked my letter, he called me. After a brief telephone conversation, we usually made a date to meet.

At first I worried about ending up having coffee with a man who turned out to be a serial killer. Although I didn't know it at the time, dating through a personal ad turned out to be tame compared to the sexualized marketplace of online dating my patients would describe to me decades later. Most of the men I met were decent. Sometimes they liked me more than I liked them; other times, the situation was reversed.

At the end of my third year of school, I met a man, William, who I dated for three months. He was a math professor and liked to do the things I enjoyed. He was kind, thoughtful, and good company. William was divorced, too, but he was eighteen years older than me with two teenagers. Over dinner, he often talked about his kids. His daughter had been accepted to an Ivy League college. His son was playing varsity soccer in high school. He was proud of both of them.

"I'd like to have a child one day, too," I said.

William looked down at his plate, buttered his bread, salted his salad, and stabbed a French fry. "I want to retire as soon as my kids are through college."

"Oh," I said.

I was disappointed, yes. Surprised? No. Our life goals didn't line up. William called me less often, and I began scanning the personal ads again.

My twenty-one-year-old self believed two people fell in love, married, and started a family. It was simple. My thirty-six-year-old self understood a relationship that led to marriage and kids was anything but. It required the alignment of many factors: mutual interest, physical chemistry, trust, getting over the baggage from past relationships, desire for kids, and shared values. A familiar thought ran through my mind. My chance of marrying and having kids felt as remote as the possibility I would one day climb Mount Everest.

The message in the popular press didn't help. In 1986, *Newsweek* magazine published an article about the likelihood of single women in their thirties marrying. The journalists reported that a thirty-year-old woman had a twenty percent chance of marrying.

The clincher was a line designed to instill fear in a female population too busy getting their careers going to find a man. Women over forty "were more likely to be killed by a terrorist" than to get married.

Newspapers and magazines across the country picked up the story. *People* magazine announced "The New Look in Old Maids," and the *New York Times* used the headline "College-Educated Women Not Married by Thirty Put on the Shelf." While the statistics were later discredited, the stories inevitably created a sense of frustration in older single women like me, who hoped they could one day marry and have a family.

———

If only I were twenty-seven, not thirty-seven. Then I would have many years left to find a partner with whom I could have a baby. But I couldn't turn the clock back. At this point, I had been yearning for a child for six years, since Tom and I started trying to conceive.

Throughout graduate school, I often considered a backup plan. I could become a single mom, having a baby through artificial insemination or adoption. More and more unmarried women were taking this route to motherhood. The census showed the number of women parenting alone increased dramatically from 3.8 million in 1970 to 6.9 million in 1980. Although most of these women were divorced, single women were also choosing to become mothers. In 1981, a psychotherapist named Jane Mattes became a single mom and created a support organization for women like herself called Single Mothers by Choice. Not surprisingly, a growing acceptance of this path to motherhood was making its way into mainstream culture. In just a few years, the idea of a single woman becoming a mom would become so widespread that Vice-President Dan Quale would criticize the TV character Murphy Brown "for mocking the importance of fathers by bearing a child alone."

My backup plan had remained on hold for the years I was in school. I didn't have the income to support a child, and I couldn't bring a baby into the home I shared with my five roommates. Graduation changed all that. A few days after the dean handed me my diploma, I began my first psychotherapy job at a drug and alcohol clinic. Four weeks later, I was sitting on the floor of my new apartment, unpacking my clothes and books.

The apartment was my first home of my own, and I was proud of it. I refurbished a dining room table with a coat of gleaming polyurethane. I bought a new futon with a pink and blue pastel-colored mattress cover that matched the ivory paint on the walls. Then, in a second-hand furniture store, I found a comfortable rocking chair for the second bedroom in my apartment, the baby's room, as I imagined it. In my mind, I was already decorating it: wallpaper with teddy bears, a softly padded changing table, and a small, colorful bureau just big enough to hold tiny clothes.

Before deciding to become a single mom, however, I wanted to talk to other women who were raising a child alone or were considering it. I joined a single mom's support group led by two unmarried social workers in their thirties who had each adopted a young boy from Colombia.

For eight weeks, I sat in a circle with five participants in the social worker's living room in her Cambridge apartment, discussing the pros and cons of becoming a single mom. Would a child do well without a father in the home? Would a close male friend be a good substitute? When the time came to tell the child about the sperm donor, what should we say? Was adoption better than artificial insemination? What about the cost? Were any of us too old to be considered adoptive parents?

As the weeks went by, the other women took tentative steps toward becoming single mothers. Sarah attended the informational meeting of several adoption agencies, and Jeanne discussed artificial insemination with her gynecologist.

I did nothing at all.

While I had become an independent and capable woman since my divorce, I still wasn't sure I could manage to raise a child on my own. I wasn't a high-energy person, as Sarah described herself. Nor did I have family close by to help me, as Jeanne did. All the women in the group already owned their own homes and were well-established in their careers. I was starting out in a new profession. In addition, maybe some of my personality characteristics would prevent me from being a patient parent. Fatigue made me irritable and short-tempered. I didn't want to mess up my little one's life.

The choice to become a single mom was far more significant than any decision I had made so far. It wasn't like going back to graduate school. Had that decision turned out to be a mistake, I could have changed my mind, dropped out, and ultimately started over again, as Joe had pointed out to me. There would be no "do-over" once I had a child in my life. Was I having a crisis of confidence or were these rational second thoughts? I couldn't tell. All I knew was the enormity of the decision was daunting.

There was also another reason I was reluctant to take a step toward becoming a single mom. I still hoped to have a loving relationship with a partner. Although bringing a child into my life wouldn't prevent me from meeting a man, it would undoubtedly make dating, already complicated enough, much more difficult. Wanting a partner embarrassed me, though. Shouldn't a woman who had accomplished as much as me—a new career, a well-paying job, my own apartment, close friends—be able to live a satisfying life without one? Sure, I could have a good life on my own. Still if I had a choice, I'd prefer a life with a loving partner rather than one alone.

I thought back to my second year of graduate school. A classmate had asked one of our instructors to describe the central issue most people brought to psychotherapy. "Love problems," he answered, without telling us if he meant love between parents and children, siblings, close friends, or romantic partners. After four years of psychotherapy training, I guessed he was referring to all these types of relationships. For me, my instructor's words carried a message I often reflected on during my years of dating: most people wanted love, and my desire for a partner was entirely normal.

Dating had become discouraging, nonetheless. The culture told me I was unlikely to get what I wanted. Still, the next time I ate lunch in the Boston College student union, I made a beeline for the *Boston Phoenix* and took one off the pile. I flipped to the classified section and ran my finger up and down the personal ads. "Single male graduate student seeks female for a long-term relationship," read a promising one. I liked academics. I wanted a serious relationship. Whoever placed this ad might be someone with whom I could get along. What would be the harm in trying again?

CHAPTER 20

ELLEN

I heard a sophisticated English accent on the other end of the telephone line the first time I talked to the graduate student seeking a long-term relationship. Bob and I agreed to meet at a coffee shop in Cambridge, and I began sizing him up as soon as we sat down. Immediately, my mental calculations about the likelihood of this date leading anywhere kicked into high gear. His friendly smile and warm brown eyes appealed to me. He was older than I expected, though, in his mid-forties, not his thirties. What was a forty-five-year-old man doing in graduate school? Shouldn't he have already figured his life out and be earning a decent salary? Had he ever been married? He hadn't mentioned a divorce on the phone. And, what about kids? Would he want them at this age?

As we sipped our coffee, Bob answered most of those questions. He had moved from England to Boston for a graduate program in sociology. Before that, he was a steward on a passenger liner in his teens and then installed telephone systems in London. He went to college in his thirties, becoming a high school teacher. When an acquaintance encouraged him to apply to graduate school in the US, he took a chance, not expecting anything would come of it. He was surprised and excited when he was accepted.

Bob intrigued me. As he told me stories about sailing around the world on the passenger ship, I checked off "traveler" on my mental list of desired male characteristics. His late-in-life career change resembled mine, making me think we might have a lot in common. The waitress brought us each a second cup of coffee, and Bob told me more about himself. He loved political films. He was doing research on young people's career fantasies. He wasn't sure he would ever move back to England.

Bob turned out to be more interesting than many men I had dated. Nonetheless, I kept waiting for him to ask me about myself, and the questions never came. I sighed as quietly as I could. My face felt as if it had frozen into a crooked smile. I poured more cream into my coffee and swished it with the spoon.

I had been on dates like this before with men who talked only about themselves, unaware of how little curiosity they exhibited about the person sitting opposite them. By the end of the date, I would feel invisible. I had spent the five years since my divorce developing a clearer and more confident sense of myself. I never wanted to feel invisible again.

When I had almost drained my cup of coffee, I glanced at Bob's watch, trying to decide how long I had to stay before I could make an excuse to leave. Finally, I mentioned a friend I needed to meet. Bob walked me to my car, where I jumped in and took off.

———————

I was discouraged. I went back to obsessing about whether I should give up dating and become a single mom. Should I have a fertility workup? What about adopting a little girl from China? I would be driving down the highway and realize I had missed my exit because I was so deep in thought. That was my state of mind when Bob called and asked if I wanted to see a movie and have dinner. Why not? It would make the time pass and distract me from a looming decision I seemed unable to make.

We sat in an Italian restaurant, sipping our wine and eating pizza. Bob talked, and I listened. I didn't let my mouth fall open into a yawn. Then, midway through our meal, he leaned toward me. "I've told you a lot about myself. Why don't you do more of the talking tonight?"

I stopped chewing. I looked at him again. In my five years of dating, no man had ever said this to me.

I talked to him about my divorce, my failed career as a historian, and my new future as a psychotherapist. I had sometimes wondered whether my two doctoral degrees would scare a man away on previous dates. Bob didn't blink an eye. Instead, he admired my willingness to start my life over again. The conversation fell into a pleasant rhythm. He listened, and I talked. Then he talked, and I listened.

Bob and I went out on dates three and four. We both liked films, museums, concerts and walking anywhere at all. Having fun was necessary at this stage of my life, and it was easy to do with Bob. Sometimes, I compared my pleasure with him to the constant low-level anxiety I had felt whenever I tried to do an activity with Tom, who constantly yawned no matter where we were and what we were doing.

For our fifth date, Bob invited me to his house for dinner. Until now, we had only met in public places. Accepting his invitation felt like a big step, a sign of increasing trust. I arrived at seven and noticed the scent of roasting meat filling the air. As we ate, the conversation became more personal than it had before. We discussed our romantic lives. I described the confusion I felt over the end of my marriage. Bob had dated many women but hadn't met anyone he wanted to live with or marry. He felt ready to settle down with someone at this point in his life.

Before I met Bob, I assumed men who reached their late thirties or early forties without having married or lived with a woman would be a poor bet for a committed relationship. The bestselling book, *The Peter Pan Syndrome*, had partly shaped this view. The gist of the book was that many men had not grown up enough—hence the Peter Pan idea—to commit to a relationship. A dermatologist I had dated fit this description. He went out with me on Friday nights and took a different woman out on Saturdays. This experience made me feel suspicious and mistrustful in a way I didn't want to repeat.

I saved the question about children for our sixth date, dinner at my apartment. Lasagna was Bob's favorite meal, and I brought out a steaming casserole dish bubbling over with cheese. Over dessert, I said I had a question for him.

"Okay," he said.

"Do you want a child in your life?" I scanned his face to look for any discomfort.

"Yes, I would."

Dinner morphed into the next morning's breakfast, and by February, Bob was calling me his girlfriend when he introduced me to his graduate school friends at a party. We must be a real couple, I thought. Then, in March, we took our first trip together. Bob had told me about two of his closest friends who had moved to Ithaca, New York. "What about a trip out to visit them?" he asked. I was stunned. This felt so different from my marriage: Tom never suggested the two of us go anywhere together and always vetoed my travel ideas.

We left on a Friday afternoon. Tiny snowflakes fell on and off during the drive, but the car was nice and warm. I navigated, and he drove. If I made a mistake and directed him down the wrong road, he just turned around and returned. No arguments. No blaming each other about who was at fault.

"We're a great team," he said on the way home from our trip.

———

Yet even after we returned from Ithaca, part of me remained tense and anxious around Bob, frightened I would miss a red flag. Like a private investigator on a case, I kept watching to see if he showed any signs of waning interest. My divorce left me feeling I should never completely let my guard down.

As the months went by, my confidence in Bob increased. He didn't cancel dates. He showed up on time. He called me every night, just like he said he would. The fact that I didn't have to guess how he would act stood in contrast to Tom, a man whose behavior I couldn't predict nor understand. Four months into my relationship with Bob, I relaxed my sensitive warning system, which felt like it had become stuck on a flashing yellow light. Then there was the night when Bob didn't phone me, as he always did.

He knew I went to bed by 10 pm. I was lying on the sofa drifting off to sleep when I noticed it was 11, and he hadn't called. I could have phoned him. But I saw his telephone calls as evidence of his continued interest in me. If he didn't call, then maybe it was waning. I swore I would never run after some man again after my experience with Tom. So, I decided to wait.

I was uncertain about what to do the next day. I thought back to how I had avoided certain topics of conversation with Tom to prevent a fight. The woman I had become in the five years since my divorce knew I shouldn't beat around the bush. I wanted my questions answered. If this relationship had a problem, I would prefer to know it sooner rather than later.

"What happened last night?" I said when he phoned me the next day. "You didn't call." I held my breath with a sense of dread. It took me a few seconds to realize I was reacting as if I were talking to my ex-husband, who became icy when I asked him a question he didn't want to answer.

"It was a busy day, and you don't stay up late. I didn't want to call and wake you up," he said.

He didn't ask me why I wanted to know. He didn't sound annoyed and didn't avoid giving me an answer. It was all so matter-of-fact: I asked a question, and he explained himself. I was overjoyed. He had passed a test I didn't even realize I was giving him.

––––––––––

I no longer feared Bob would walk out the door and disappear when we disagreed. If I suspected something was bothering him, I could ask him how he felt, rather than guess, as I had often done with Tom. Being with Bob felt so easy and uncomplicated. Bit by bit, I dismantled the wall I had built to protect myself from being hurt again. Sometimes in the morning, I rolled over to look at him and watched him sleep, feeling warm and cozy. I was falling in love, but I couldn't tell if Bob was falling in love with me.

On beautiful days, we would walk along the Charles River in Cambridge, and I imagined we reached the perfect spot for him to declare his love for me. Yet he never said anything about love or any of his feelings toward me. We had been dating for a year. Shouldn't he have said something by now?

Unsure of what to do, I weighed my alternatives in bed at night when I couldn't sleep. I could wait, continue dating him, and see if he told me he loved me. That plan was risky. I might end up being hurt and blindsided as I had been with Tom. If Bob didn't care as much as I hoped he did, I wanted to know now. The alternative required courage. I would have to speak up and ask what he felt towards me. In other words, use the voice I had been building up since my divorce.

The next week, Bob and I sat at a picnic table in a park, having lunch on a bright, sunny fall day. I took a napkin out of my lunch bag, folded it and unfolded it several times. I picked up my sandwich and put it down. Suddenly, I couldn't stand not knowing his feelings for me for one more minute.

"I have something I want to ask you," I said.

"Sure," he said.

I stared at an ant slowly crawling on the ground for a few seconds. Then I looked up at Bob. "I've been curious about what you feel for me. You never talk about it."

There was a long pause. He started a sentence and stopped midway through. He tried a second time.

"I care for you. Definitely," Bob said. "I'm not sure I am in love with you."

My face felt hot, and my chest hurt. The man I had been dating for a year just said the words I was most afraid of hearing. I thought of just walking away. Before I could stand up, Bob began to talk again.

"I thought if I fell in love with a woman, I would think about her all the time, feel swept away by her. It's not that way with you."

Neither of us said anything. Finally, I swallowed hard and forced myself to speak. "If you don't feel whatever you hoped to feel for me now, it's unlikely to come later," I said. Bob didn't reply.

I stood up and shoved my sandwich into a paper bag, taking a few steps toward my car. "It's best to stop seeing each other," I said. From the corner of my eye, I registered a look of shock on his face. After that, I had only one thought: I must leave Bob before he left me. Later I would understand I was reacting like a woman whose past trauma had triggered a fight or flight response; the pain, fear, and suspicion I carried from my divorce still affected me in ways I couldn't control. When I finally got to my car, I slumped into the driver's seat and sobbed.

The night felt as sad as any night since Tom had left me. I couldn't eat. I couldn't sleep. I lay on the sofa, rereading the sections on grief in *Crazy Time* that had comforted me through my divorce. The book reminded me I got over Tom. Eventually, I would get over Bob, too.

When I got home from work the next evening, I saw my answering machine's bright red, blinking light. I tapped the switch on and Bob's deep voice, "Please call me as soon as you get in" came through. An hour later, we sat on opposite ends of my living room sofa. Bob glanced at the floor before he looked up at me.

"I want us to stay together," he said.

"What about not loving me?" I asked.

"It's not that I don't love you."

"What is it then?"

"I thought falling in love with the right woman would be like a movie: two people locked eyes across a room and knew they were meant for each other, passionate, all-consuming. It's not like that with you."

"Why do you want to stay together?" I asked.

"I like what we have. It's the kind of relationship I want. We get along well, we're attracted to one another, we share values. Even before I met you, I realized real love wasn't going to be like it was in the movies."

I didn't know what to think. I had expected a relationship would progress from increasing trust and involvement in one another's lives, as ours had done, to a starry-eyed declaration of love. I wasn't going to get this from Bob. He cared for me in his way. As I thought about it, his feelings for me were similar to the ones I felt for him: a gentle and warm affection, a slow burn rather than a bonfire. Maybe people loved each other differently when they were older. This could be a mature, grown-up kind of love that Bob had made his peace with. Could I do that, too?

"I'm afraid of getting hurt again," I said.

Perhaps Bob was settling for me temporarily, and when he met the woman of his dreams, he would leave me for her. Maybe I was settling for less than I wanted in a relationship. I had made this mistake once and didn't want to repeat it. I studied Bob's face, hoping it would reveal his true intentions.

"I'm reserved about my feelings," he said. "A lot of Englishmen are."

I watched Bob, and my brain replayed a conversation we had had at a restaurant two weeks earlier. I was raving about the lobster. "How's your meal?" I asked.

"Okay."

"You don't like it?"

"No, I do," he said. "It's okay."

"You told me lasagna is your favorite."

"It is," Bob said, "The food's okay."

The fact we spoke the same language made me overlook our cultural differences about how we expressed our emotions.

The sofa creaked as Bob leaned closer to me. "Maybe if I made more of a commitment, you would be less scared," he said.

"Like what?"

"What about moving in together?"

I felt as if I was teetering back and forth on the edge of a cliff. Whatever Bob hadn't said in words, he said in his actions for the year I had known him. I might never get a chance like this again. Deciding to live with him would be a risk. Breaking up with him would be a risk, too.

Bob looked worried and serious. This would be an important step for him. He had never been married. He had never even lived with a woman before. Maybe he was frightened, too. He inched closer to me, closing the gap between us. "What do you think about looking for an apartment together next week?" he asked.

Without thinking, I tilted my head towards his. "Yes," I said.

CHAPTER 21

MEGHAN

On a cold February morning, a slick coat of ice covered the walkway that led from my car to the office. I inched along the sidewalk, almost losing my footing. It was school vacation week, and Meghan was coming in for an early morning appointment. I didn't want to be late.

When she showed up, she was dressed like me: fuzzy winter boots, slacks, and a scratchy wool sweater. I smiled hello, and she nodded back to me. She looked miserable. "How did the week go?" I asked.

There were the usual frustrations with her students at school. Her daughter was coming down with another cold. Meghan had the sniffles, too. She paused and sighed. Both of us were quiet. The corners of her mouth sank into a deep frown. I let the silence continue uninterrupted for another ten seconds, aware of the difference between the rhythm of a therapy session and an ordinary social conversation. As a psychotherapist, I often let the silence linger, sensing the patient needed the time and space to put a challenging experience into words.

"The marriage?" I asked, thinking a gentle nudge might help her open up. Meghan nodded.

I felt a familiar pull to find something to say, anything really, that would make everything better. I also knew it wasn't my job right now. What comforting statement could I make anyway? Meghan faced a hard, difficult choice. Nothing I could do would make the decision any less painful. Finally, she leaned forward.

"I can't make myself love Patrick," Meghan said. "I wish I could. I just can't."

I remained silent again, waiting to see if she had more to add. Meghan was quiet, too. "I know that is difficult for you to admit," I said.

Then, like a lawyer presenting evidence to support her case, she listed all their unsuccessful efforts to improve the marriage. Counseling hadn't worked, neither had their brief separation. They weren't having sex. They were barely speaking to one another.

"Here is what I want to understand," Meghan said.

I sat up straight to see what would come next.

"What is a good reason for a divorce?" she asked.

The expression on her face told me she was asking herself the question, not me. Still, her query got me thinking. Certain circumstances made the answer clear-cut; I knew that from treating patients for thirty years. I thought about Lisa. Greg's adultery gave her an acceptable reason to leave him, yet even she had struggled over the decision for many months.

Meghan's decision would have been much easier if Patrick had been unfaithful. She could have left her husband without a glance backward. If he had been physically abusive, she wouldn't have doubted she had made the right decision to end the marriage. Her friends and family would have supported her, too. I could even picture them slapping her on the back as if she had kicked a soccer ball right into the middle of the goal. She would be a woman who hadn't let herself be victimized by a man, a heroine.

What about the woman who left a decent guy because she didn't love him? This type of decision was far more complicated. Leaving her husband gave her another chance at a happier life. Yet there was a price to pay. She had to accept her choice would hurt him and, more importantly, her innocent little girl. As a mother and teacher, Meghan always worked hard to improve youngsters' lives. Now she was torn; part of her was drawn to the possibility of a more satisfying future, and the other part uncertain if it was worth sacrificing her daughter's happiness for her own.

Had Meghan been a student in one of the history courses I had taught years earlier, I would have explained that Americans' ideas about a good reason for divorce had changed over time. Before the late 1960s, married men and women needed to demonstrate cruelty or adultery to have the court grant a divorce. Love didn't enter into the discussion. The law changed in the 1970s, as society no longer tried to deter the end of a marriage through legal means. California became the first state to move to no-fault divorce in 1970, and many states followed suit within the next decade. At this point in history, it was enough to claim irreconcilable differences when you wanted to get a divorce. From a legal point of view, Meghan's reason for divorcing her husband—she no longer loved him—was enough.

I was Meghan's therapist, however, not her history professor. And I certainly wasn't her attorney. She understood both her husband and daughter would be hurt if she decided to end her marriage. Did she want me to give her permission to decide to put her own needs before theirs? I knew it would make it easier if I could tell her what to do. That might be a job for the priest at her church, not me. As a therapist, my role was to encourage her to think for herself.

Meghan's conflict reminded me of some of my other female patients who struggled to balance their personal needs with the needs of others. For example, twenty-eight-year-old Sarina described the pull she felt between her mom's plea that Sarina buy a house close to where her mother lived rather than move to a more affordable home thirty minutes to the north. Another patient, Tamara, thirty-two years old with a four-month-old baby, discussed the uncertainty she felt about returning to work after her son's birth. She couldn't decide if she should put her infant in daycare or stay home with him, sacrificing her career as a biological researcher she had taken a decade to build.

I listened to these women struggle with their dilemma and thought about Carol Gilligan's work on female psychology. Gilligan asked girls and women to talk through an important moral decision. Her discoveries mirrored those of Bob Kegan, my former professor and her colleague at Harvard.

Gilligan's subjects displayed two different ways of dealing with this dilemma. The first way, what Gilligan called the conventional level, referred to subjects who made their decision about what was right and wrong based on whether or not it pleased people in their lives. In other words, they did what their parents or boyfriend wanted them to, just as Kegan's socialized self did. Gilligan called the second way of decision-making the post-conventional level, and it mirrored Kegan's self-authored self. These subjects considered their own needs, not just the needs of others as they decided what to do. The shift from conventional to post-conventional was a sign of growth, an ability to think more complexly. As any therapist can attest though, change is not easy, nor does it stick to a particular timetable. Meghan's struggle over the decision to divorce was a case in point.

For much of the winter, she remained paralyzed. Her paralysis reminded me of Lisa, at a standstill for many months, unable to divorce Greg. Both women's struggles highlighted the agony of the decision to divorce, a fact I brought up at a dinner party when one of my guests launched into a rant about how quickly couples seemed to split up today. I had heard this sentiment before and knew where my guest was headed: people today aren't committed enough to their marriages. I once believed this myself. However, I didn't any longer and saw this as a sign of my development as a therapist. I blurted out what I thought. "Very few people divorce their spouses quickly. They live in unhappy marriages for a long time. Believe me. The decision to divorce is a long and painful one."

———

On a late February afternoon, Meghan sat in my office and said, "There is no way I can end my marriage without hurting Patrick and my daughter. I picture his eyes welling up if I tell him I want a divorce. Then I think about how our little girl will cry when Patrick isn't living at the house. It breaks my heart."

I waited to see if she would backtrack again, telling me the situation wasn't that bad. Instead, the competent, teachery side of Meghan came out, and she wanted to know my professional opinion about the impact of divorce on kids. "What do you think it will do to my daughter if we split up?" she asked. Her voice had an unfamiliar shaky sound.

Many patients had asked me this question before. The research showed in the short run, children may have a difficult time. "It wouldn't be surprising if your little girl showed separation anxiety and became clingy and tearful when you dropped her at daycare," I said. In the long run, however, most kids re-established their equilibrium following their parents' divorce, returning to their prior level of functioning once they got used to the new family arrangement. So kids whose grades dropped right after their mom and dad separated later raised them again, and boys and girls who showed more behavioral problems, tantrums for the little ones or argumentativeness for the bigger ones, settled down, too.

There was a critical exception to this broad generalization. When there were high levels of animosity in the divorce and children were put in the middle, they couldn't recover. As a result, kids' well-being depended on whether parents were mature enough to put their offspring's needs before the impulse to exact revenge on their spouse. One of my former teenage patients came to mind. She lived with her dad who constantly demeaned the girl's mother. As a result, my patient's grades dropped, and she spent most of the days in her room with the door shut, refusing to come out when her mom came to pick her up for a visit. I worried about the girl. The mother was heartbroken. The only person who seemed unperturbed was the father who regaled me with stories about his wife leaving him for another man.

––––––––––

My conversations with patients often made me question my thinking, and the months I spent discussing Meghan's marriage with her were no different. Many of our talks made me aware of how my ideas about divorce had changed over time. When I started my clinical practice, I was very sensitive to people who had been betrayed by their spouses or left by them. I identified with these patients. Maybe even too much. My personal history made it easy to understand their pain. This history, however, made it difficult for me to empathize with the other kinds of patients— the unhappily married ones who wanted to leave their spouses. I would wonder why they hadn't worked harder at keeping their marriages together. The circumstances almost didn't matter. But over time, my attitude changed.

As an individual and a marital therapist, I treated men and women who were deeply unhappy in their marriages. They had tried to make the relationship work, sometimes for years. Too many years, I decided after I watched the lines of strain etched in their faces grow deeper. Encouraging them to stay in a miserable situation was not helping them. From a clinical point of view, they needed to consider both alternatives: remain married or divorce.

As I listened to patient after patient wading through the painful decision about ending their marriage, I often thought about Tom. Shouldn't he have had a second chance at happiness if I wasn't the right woman for him? Leaving me was the right thing for him to do. He didn't deserve a lifetime of disappointment in marriage any more than Meghan did. It wasn't fair to him. Ultimately, I realized it wouldn't have been fair to me either. I deserved better than to be married to a man who didn't want to be with me.

Winter loosened its grip, and tiny pale green leaves covered the tree branches outside my office window. Meghan was still going back and forth about her marriage. She knew in her heart she didn't love Patrick, and she didn't want to be married to him. "I want to want him," she told me one day in a voice shot through with regret. "But I don't."

In late April, Meghan finally found a way to make her decision. She realized she wasn't doing Patrick any favors by not telling him the truth. He should have the chance to find a woman who loved him, not simply tolerated him. Over the next few weeks, Meghan and I discussed this idea more. Finally, she said her daughter deserved to see parents who loved each other, not two people simply rotating around each other in their separate orbits.

Perhaps by now, Patrick knew what was coming. When Meghan told him she wanted to divorce, he wasn't surprised. After she put her daughter to bed one night, they sat at the kitchen table and made their decisions amicably. Patrick would move out and buy a condo close by. They would have joint custody of their daughter. When it came to money, they agreed to split everything in half. They were much more decent to each other than many divorcing couples I had seen, leaving me optimistic that their toddler would thrive despite the short-term disruption in her life.

It was June, and Meghan's school year had already ended. She came in for her appointment wearing her shorts again and her hair in a ponytail. We agreed it had been such a challenging year for her. She looked forward to a summer without teaching. Mostly she was relieved her divorce would soon be final.

Over the next hour, we talked about the future. Meghan still hoped to move from teaching into educational administration. While she wanted a romantic partner, she had no interest in ever getting married again. Once was enough. She had accepted the possibility she might not have a second child, although she hadn't ruled out adopting a kid later in her life. It looked like she had given up on the checklists she had relied upon for years.

This was the new Meghan.

The insights we had discussed during her year of psychotherapy threaded themselves through the conversation. Plans don't always work out the way we want them to. It's possible to accept uncertainty. Solutions in life turned out to be less precise than any math problem Meghan had tried to solve. It is okay to admit you have less control over the outcome of your life than you imagined. Feelings are important, so don't ignore them. Of course, I didn't tell Meghan what I was thinking as we discussed her progress: I was describing my "adulting" process, as much as I was summing up hers.

We weren't terminating, just going from biweekly therapy to monthly check-ins. A "tune-up," as my patient Janet called it. Before Meghan left that day, I asked her if she wanted to hear a personal anecdote. I wasn't surprised when she said "yes." In over thirty years of practicing psychotherapy, no one ever declined my offer. "When I was a teenager," I said, "I believed grown-ups knew what they were doing. Of course, I thought I would also know what I was doing as an adult. By the time I got into my thirties, I felt so uncertain I wondered if I had missed some important life lesson everyone else had received. Thirty years of practice have made me see it differently. We are all bumbling around in life. That's as good as it gets."

CHAPTER 22

LISA

I thought I knew everything about Lisa there was to know. She had been in therapy with me for almost a year and had told me so many stories about her life. Nevertheless, Lisa hadn't made the progress she had hoped to make. Most importantly, she hadn't called an attorney, despite the number of months she thought about it, and I guessed there was more I needed to understand about her. So, I decided to go back over Lisa's family history to uncover clues I might have missed.

"Does your fear about getting divorced feel familiar to you?" I asked. "Does it bring you back to an earlier part of your life?"

"It makes me think of my parents' divorce," she said. It was a story she had told me before. Her dad had had an affair for years, and he hid it well. Still, she wasn't sure whether or not her mom knew about it. Or maybe her mom didn't want to know what was going on.

Perhaps the tone in Lisa's voice when she suggested her mom avoided the signs of her dad's infidelity—the nights he came home late, the unexplained errands lasting hours in the middle of the day—made me sit up straight and take notice. I assumed her mother had grown sick of her husband's unfaithfulness and finally divorced him. Now, as I listened to Lisa, it occurred to me I had never asked whether this was actually the case.

"Did she finally kick your dad out?" I said.

Lisa didn't say anything for a few seconds. I glanced at her face, trying to picture how innocent she must have looked at age fifteen when her parents' marriage was falling apart. Teenagers were still so impressionable.

"No," she said. "She would have never done that. She was afraid to be alone without my dad. He finally left her and married his girlfriend. My mother never really recovered. She didn't date. She had few friends. She didn't have much of a life."

Her voice trailed off. For a few seconds, neither of us said anything. Lisa's shoulders sagged like a heavy weight hung around her neck. She was looking at the floor when she started to talk again.

"One of those times I kicked Greg out of the house because of the cheating," Lisa said, "he told me that without him, I would end up like my mom." A flash of pain crossed her face as if she had just ripped a bandage off her arm and was showing me a deep gash. Greg knew her well and didn't hesitate to go for the most vulnerable parts of her psyche.

I was beginning to understand Lisa's dilemma more clearly. To divorce Greg meant she would turn into a lonely woman, as she believed her mother had become, unable to put her life back together. On the other hand, to stay with him was to make the same choice her mom had made, tolerating an unfaithful husband for many years. Lisa didn't want to end up like her mom, yet she couldn't see any alternative. No wonder she had remained paralyzed for so long.

"You don't sound anything like your mother," I said.

"Really?"

"I have known you for almost a year. You have close friends. You love your job. The teacher you work with admires how you handle the students. That sounds pretty different from your mom."

Lisa smiled a little; I wasn't sure she believed me. I thought back to the research on women's lack of self-confidence which explained why I could see her strengths and she couldn't.

"Your mother wasn't a great role model," I said, concerned I might sound too harsh. But at this point in treatment, being blunt felt worth the risk of potentially offending Lisa with my criticism of her mom. I wanted to show her that the source of her paralysis lay in her family situation.

"I know," Lisa said. "Not a great role model at all."

The psychologist John D. Mayer pointed out that parental role models offer children a picture of who they might become. Lisa's vision of her future self was a mother who seemed barely able to manage her life once her husband had left her. Her mom lacked self-confidence. Lisa did too. To move forward with her divorce, Lisa needed an image of herself as a single woman thriving independently. This new picture came from a surprising story she revealed soon after.

On a July day, Lisa was in my office talking about money. She had returned to this topic many times since I had known her, as women who made far less than their husbands often did when contemplating a divorce. So far, Greg had continued to cover the mortgage and the household expenses. Since they weren't divorced, she feared he would stop paying one day and there would be nothing she could do about it. I thought back to Lisa's work life, remembering her years as a stay-at-home mom and how little money she made when she took a job as a teacher's aide. It struck me that I didn't understand why she became an aide in the first place.

"How did you end up getting your job?" I asked.

"We needed my salary and health insurance," she said. "I only took the position because Greg went to prison."

I had glanced out my office window a few seconds earlier, and my head jerked back towards Lisa. My eyes opened wide.

"Prison?" I said. "Greg went to prison?"

Lisa nodded.

I clamped down on my jaw to keep it from dropping open. He was a successful businessman living in the middle-class town where I practiced. I had imagined him in a tailored three-piece suit and now had to change the picture to an orange jumpsuit.

Lisa began to speak more slowly, choosing her words carefully. White-collar crime was all she would say when I asked her why Greg ended up incarcerated. They paid lawyers a lot of money and fought it for quite a while. Finally, there was a trial, and he was sentenced to prison for a year. Lisa needed a salary and health insurance. The children were teenagers, old enough to take care of themselves, so she got her job as a teacher's aide.

I interrupted her at this point in the conversation. "What was your life like when Greg was in prison?" I asked. "Didn't you have to manage things on your own?"

Lisa agreed. She paid all the family bills, handled the house repairs, and disciplined the kids. She mowed the lawn in the summer. In the winter, she shoveled snow. I listened to Lisa recite everything she had done and felt like scratching my head, thinking about how to help her see how competent she was.

"You know, you keep worrying about how you would survive alone, without Greg," I said. "The truth is you did fine when he was in prison, and you have been doing fine by yourself for the past five months."

She let fifteen seconds of silence go by before she said anything. "I hadn't thought of it that way until you said it," she replied.

For a psychotherapist, there are no better words to hear.

Over the next month, Lisa told me more stories about her achievements rather than her flaws. She had kept life moving along for her kids when Greg was in prison. Even though she never expected to work outside the home, she discovered she loved her job and was good at it.

The stories we tell about our lives shape the choices we make. Psychologist Dan P. McAdams summed up the significance of life stories. He suggested that narratives inform how we view ourselves in the past and in the future. Lisa's new stories highlighted the strengths she had previously ignored. They contained the message she could meet challenges she thought she couldn't meet.

In October, fifteen months after I first met her, Lisa hired an attorney. She described the meetings with her lawyer and told me how uncertain she felt about making decisions about her financial situation in the divorce. Should she buy Greg out of his share of the house or wait until she sold it? Go for alimony or half of his retirement money? She trusted her attorney's advice, but she was the one who had the final say. Despite her anxieties about the decisions, however, Lisa felt more empowered. She used the words "standing up to Greg" as she told me about the process of getting divorced.

At this point, Lisa switched from biweekly therapy to monthly appointments. It took six months to iron out the financial issues and finalize the divorce. During this time, she still worried about whether ending the marriage was the right decision, and I often reminded her how this divorce had changed her for the better. "You would have remained the scared woman you were when I first met you. Not the competent version of yourself you have become now," I said.

Lisa saw the transformation in herself. However, an undercurrent of sadness and regret never entirely left her. It went back to her kids. More than anything, she had wanted to give them what she never had: a mother and father who loved each other and lived together always. If it weren't for the choice Greg made, she would have been able to do it. For that, she would never forgive him for as long as she lived.

"I understand," I said. "There will always be a part of you wishing your life turned out differently."

Twenty months after I first met her, Lisa was legally divorced. She was nervous on the day of her divorce hearing and had to remind herself she had done nothing wrong. After the hearing, she went home to her kids. They weren't happy with the new family arrangement. None of them liked Greg's girlfriend, and they wouldn't visit their dad when she was there.

After she was divorced, Lisa went on a date with a man she met through a friend. She liked him and could tell he liked her, too. He had already called her to see if they could have dinner together next week.

This therapy session felt different. The pressure was gone. The conversation felt like two friends catching up. She planned to take her children to the Cape for a week and asked me where I would travel next. I answered her question without doing the old therapist trick of inquiring about why she had asked. I had been here many times with other patients, and I could guess what was coming next. Finally, she was ready to terminate treatment.

"I thought I would stop therapy for a while," she said.

"Sure. Why not? You are doing great," I said.

I thought back to my hesitation when she had ended therapy a year earlier. There was none of that now. I trusted Lisa to see she had made sufficient progress. We chatted for another five minutes. I glanced at the clock and repeated the statement I had said at the end of each therapy session for almost two years. "Looks like we'll have to stop." This time I heard a little crack in my voice and wondered if Lisa heard it, too. "You can always come back," I said.

"I know," she said. Then I hugged her, and she walked out the door.

CHAPTER 23

ELLEN

"Y ou really look pregnant," Joe, my therapist, said. "How far along?"

The corners of my mouth slid up into a wide grin. "Five months. I'm due in May."

"Wow," he said, beaming back at me.

I had last seen Joe two years earlier when I first started dating Bob. At that point, Joe and I had discussed work problems, how stuck I felt at my job, not romantic difficulties. The last he knew, I was beginning to go out with someone with whom I got along well.

I quickly gave him the abbreviated update: the personal ad that introduced Bob to me, the fun we had together, our shared values. "He even likes to travel," I said, aware of a sparkle of surprise in my voice about finding a man who wanted to see the world with me. Finally, I told Joe we had been living together for almost a year after we had dated for the same amount of time.

"Everything sounds perfect," he said. "So, what brings you back?"

"Well, Bob and I have been talking about getting married. He wants to do it, and I don't know if marriage is for me."

I first told Bob we couldn't get married because I was still considering adopting a child, and marriage could make adoption difficult. The agencies had many regulations about who could and couldn't adopt. Bob's age might disqualify him right from the outset. It would be easier to adopt if I were single. Now, since we were going to have our own baby, everything had changed. The reason for putting off marriage had disappeared, and Bob wanted to go ahead with a wedding. I wasn't sure. The statistics about remarriage were so discouraging: sixty percent of second marriages ended in divorce compared to fifty percent of first marriages.

"Why don't you want to get married?" Joe asked.

"I'm afraid."

"Of what?" he said.

"Getting divorced again."

The logical part of me understood a break-up would be hard whether we were married or not. Nothing could prevent that. But the part of me still scarred from the end of my marriage to Tom worried that divorce could add so many more complicated layers and varieties of pain: the humiliating acknowledgement that yes this was a second divorce; exorbitant attorney fees; and how the court would regulate the division of assets. Now, with a child coming, I would have to grapple with custody laws.

The only way to ensure I would never get divorced was never get married.

I settled back against Joe's sofa and looked around his office. Nothing had changed since I was last here. The toys were still in

one corner, the desk piled high with books in the other. I was sitting in the same spot I always sat, and Joe had settled himself in
his usual blue chair. He leaned forward in his familiar pose: arms
on his knees and clasped hands together. I could still smell his
aftershave—sweet, comforting, familiar.

"Wait a second," he said. "What happened to your plan to
adopt a baby?"

I told him my support group had met monthly for the past
three years. Two of the women had already adopted kids. From
them, I learned how hard it was to adopt: the cost was high, and
there was a very long wait for a child. "To tell the truth, it was
daunting," I said. "Once I had a partner, I realized I wanted to try
to have a baby of our own."

On a warm spring night nine months earlier, Bob had taken
me out for dinner for my thirty-ninth birthday in mid-April.
The conversation drifted from a film we both wanted to see to
our delicious meal. Nevertheless, in the back of my mind, I was
thinking about how I was thirty-nine, and I still hadn't had a
baby. I didn't even know if I could get pregnant. I was seven years
older than my last unsuccessful effort to conceive with Tom.

While Bob had already told me he wanted to have children,
we had never discussed when to start trying. I wondered if he just
wanted a theoretical infant, not a real one. Would he pull a Tom
and change his mind at the last moment?

"We need to talk," I finally said when we got home that night.

"About what?" he asked.

"Kids," I said,

"What about kids?"

"I just turned thirty-nine. If we really want to try to have a baby, then we shouldn't put it off any longer."

Neither of us said anything for a few seconds.

"Well, I still have my dissertation to finish," he said.

As soon as those words left his mouth, my heart sank. I felt as if I were time-traveling back to the night Tom had told me he decided he didn't want a child. Those memories lay right below the surface of my consciousness, ready to spring out at any time. Suddenly, I felt like I was back in the situation I had been determined to avoid. I immediately decided Bob was just another man who wouldn't stay around to have a baby. As part of me imagined the worst-case scenario—he would pack up his things and move out, just as my ex-husband did—anger grew inside me. I wasn't panic-stricken, like with Tom. I had left the woman I had been back then far behind.

I was pissed.

I took a deep breath and tried to calm down. I knew the advice I would have given any woman or man I saw in psychotherapy. Don't let your past experiences color your present reaction. Get the facts before you jump to any conclusions. Ask your partner questions and listen carefully to his answers. Be patient. It can take a long time for two people to understand one another.

"So, what do you want to do?" I asked, forcing my voice into a neutral tone I didn't feel.

"I don't know," he replied. "Come on. We can figure something out."

Bob's words calmed me down. His reaction differed from Tom, who shut down any difficult conversation. Once I stopped panicking, I began to think more clearly. My brain shifted into planning mode.

"What about this," I said. "When do you think you will finish your dissertation?"

"About a year from now," he told me.

I took out my appointment book with next year's calendar at the back. I counted backward nine months from next May. If we started trying to get pregnant this August, five months from now, that would be the soonest we would have a baby. Even then, the chance of conceiving the first time we tried seemed slim.

"Sounds good," he said. "We've got a plan."

No argument. No equivocating.

As I told the story, Joe leaned further forward in the chair.

"Then what?" he asked.

"Anyway, we started trying to conceive in August. It simply didn't occur to me it would work. Then I got pregnant the first month we tried. So, I came back for your opinion," I finally said to Joe. "About marriage."

"What do you want to know?" he asked.

I stopped to think about how to put my question into words. I wanted a crystal ball, someone to tell me if I married a second time, would I divorce a second time, too? Without a guarantee, it seemed impossible to take another chance. Joe couldn't give me the assurance about the future I wanted. Of course, I knew that all along. Still, he was a much more seasoned clinician than I was. I had only been practicing psychotherapy for three years and hadn't treated many couples. I asked him what would make it less likely a couple would end up divorced.

"How they fight with each other is crucial," he answered without missing a beat. "What about you and Bob? What are your fights like?"

I described our first fight shortly after we moved in together. I woke up on Valentine's Day expecting to see a card on the kitchen table. Apart from the lonely-looking salt and pepper shakers, nothing was there. Maybe Bob would bring home candy or flowers after work. But he walked in the door empty-handed. So, I gave him his card and asked why he hadn't gotten me one.

"It is a ridiculous holiday. It is completely commercialized."

"I don't care," I said. "It means a lot to me."

We went back and forth several times, our voices getting louder and sharper. I told him he had been inconsiderate. He accused me of being "too sensitive." He might as well have waved a red flag in front of a bull. Who was he to decide which of my feelings were too sensitive?

Bob told me he was done talking. Then he walked away. I heard the sharp slapping sound his shoes made against the wood floor in our apartment. It felt like a déjà vu. I might as well have been living with my ex-husband. The whole scene conjured up Tom's iciness when he was angry with me.

Bob slept like a log, as he always did, and I tossed and turned most of the night. The next morning I was waiting for him at the kitchen table when he woke up. He made a cup of coffee and sat down across from me.

"Do you want to talk about the fight?" I asked. He nodded "yes." We were both calmer now. I told him a card on Valentine's Day meant something to me, even if he thought it was ridiculous. We didn't have to agree on the meaning of this holiday. I just wanted him to respect my point of view. He told me he understood. Although I wouldn't know it then, he would never miss giving me a card on Valentine's Day for the next thirty years.

"You have a good process," Joe told me when I finished talking.

"What do you mean?'

"You work out your disagreements in a pretty effective way. Fights don't escalate too much. You don't say hurtful things to each other you might regret. Once you calm down, you try to talk rationally to each other. That tells me you and Bob have many more skills to sustain a marriage than you and Tom had."

I thought about what Joe was saying. When I married Tom, I believed love was enough to keep us together. However, Joe was looking at marriage from a different angle. After years of working with couples, he understood how two people needed to talk to one another to iron out their differences.

"That doesn't guarantee anything," I finally said.

"You are right. No guarantees."

He hugged me goodbye and walked me to the door. I thought about the many therapy sessions when he had seen me at my worst. All those hours I had spent on that sofa, sobbing, describing my fears, wondering if I would feel anything other than despair. Today's session made me feel as if I had recounted the unexpected twist to a novel, the surprise happy ending of a sad story. When I looked at the smile on Joe's face, I could see he was pleased, too.

———

I left Joe's office still uncertain about what to do. For old-time's sake, I walked to the town library where I had often gone years earlier after my therapy appointments. The library hadn't changed any more than Joe's office. The same hushed silence floated in the air, and the slightly musty odor of old books still hung in the stacks.

As I curled up in one of the comfortable chairs, I thought about what had changed since I sat here years ago. My relationship with Bob was different from the one I had had with Tom. We were more connected, sharing values and interests my ex-husband and I never had. Plus, Bob was a talker, putting his feelings into words in a way my ex-husband never could. He was also a careful listener. And he recognized if we didn't discuss our disagreements, we would never resolve anything. Our "process," as Joe called it, *was* a good one. I could see it now.

It wasn't just that I was marrying a different kind of man; I had changed, too. I had lived by myself for two years before Bob and I moved in together, and I was no longer afraid of being alone. I received a glowing evaluation in my staff psychology position. I was making more money than I had ever made and intended never to depend on a man financially again. I was excited about becoming a mom. While I had the normal jitters of any first-time mother-to-be, I also felt confident I could manage raising a child. I had fully "adulted," although I wouldn't know that word until Meghan introduced me to it twenty-five years later.

Then there were significant internal changes. I listened to what my body was telling me about my emotions. If something Bob said hurt my feelings, I tried to understand what was bothering me. Once I figured it out, I would talk to him about it. I was no longer afraid to speak up.

Finally, I had learned to accept uncertainty—the same lesson my patient Meghan would eventually learn. I changed careers from history professor to psychologist, not knowing how it would work. Why couldn't I get married with unanswered questions about my future? That was all everyone did anyway, whether they recognized it or not. In the end, I knew I could survive a divorce. That was another change, too. I had done it once, and if I had to, I would do it again. As my patient Lisa would learn years later, in the face of divorce, you will discover strengths you didn't know you had.

Before I left the library, I walked up the stairs to the second floor, where I knew the books on marriage stood. The book *Crazy Time* with its familiar cover caught my eye. As happy as I was to see it, I hoped I wouldn't need it again.

I went out to my car to head home. Bob and I lived in the same town I had lived in with Tom, so I took a short detour to drive past my old apartment, still painted its unattractive pale yellow. When I had lived on this street eight years earlier, I thought my marriage to Tom was good, and I couldn't figure out why he didn't see it, too. As the years passed, I completely rewrote the story. Now it looked like there were many problems in that relationship I had been reluctant to acknowledge because of my fear of being alone. In this new version of my story, Tom had turned out to be the brave one, ending a marriage that should never have taken place. By divorcing me, he had done me the most significant favor anyone had ever done.

My second wedding turned out to be nothing like my first. Having already dished out a lot of money for my first one, my father made a limited financial investment. Maybe he wanted to see if this marriage would last. "I'll pay for the booze," he said when Bob and I announced our intention to wed. A justice of the peace had married me and Tom. For the second wedding, I wanted a rabbi to marry us under the traditional Jewish canopy, just in case a God's presence might bless this marriage and arrange its success.

"What about a pre-wedding honeymoon, before I am too pregnant to travel?" I said to Bob. With the similar conversation I had with Tom in my mind, I still wasn't apprehensive. Bob and I had traveled as much as possible in the two years we had been together. Since our budget was tight, we got an inexpensive flight for a three-night trip to New Orleans. We split our time between a cheap hotel and one night in a fancy inn. Breakfast was often just a cup of coffee and a sweet beignet, with a splurge at an elegant French restaurant for dinner one night.

One afternoon after we returned home, we took a walk in Boston and passed by the Copley Square Hotel. "Let's go there for our wedding night," Bob said. I was so taken aback I couldn't figure out what to say. We had already spent money on what had been our honeymoon. Shouldn't we be economizing since we were about to have a baby? Marrying a man who wanted to celebrate our wedding twice felt like an embarrassment of riches.

Bob and I married in February, two and a half months before our son was born. My parents walked me down the aisle. Friends held up the canopy we stood under to take our vows. The rabbi, who never once mentioned my pregnancy, cracked a few jokes. Bob quipped back a funny retort. I could feel my eyes begin to well up: the people who were witnessing this marriage—my loving family and friends who had accompanied me on a journey that began when Tom left and through the years it took to put my life back together—were with me still. Only Joe wasn't there. While I didn't know it at the time, there would be plenty of opportunities to describe the scene at one of the many appointments I would have with him over the next twenty-five years.

Bob and I stood under the canopy, and he leaned down to give me a tender kiss. The rabbi placed the wine glass we both sipped from into a paper bag. I heard the loud crunch of my new husband's foot landing on the bag and crushing the glass.

"Mazel tov," my father called out. "Mazel tov."

CHAPTER 24

MEGHAN, LISA, AND ELLEN

In early March 2020, at the start of the pandemic, I closed my psychotherapy office and offered my patients the choice of therapy on the phone or online. Meghan chose the phone. For the following two years, she discussed the challenges of being divorced. When she did, I thought about Sigmund Freud's view that work and love were central to our experience of being human. As a newly single woman, Meghan needed to figure out both aspects of her life.

After fifteen years as a classroom teacher, she felt burnt out. She wondered if this was the right time to move into educational administration, as she always assumed she would. "My daughter is still so young," she said. "I planned to wait until she was older to make a career change." Then, in the spring of 2022, an assistant principal position unexpectedly opened up at a nearby school, and she contemplated whether she should apply for this job.

"What is the harm in trying?" I asked.

Two days later, she sent her application to the school superintendent. She breezed through the job interview, just as I expected. The superintendent offered her the position the next week. If anyone was destined to be a successful school principal, it was Meghan; she was firm, capable, and clear about her expectations of students.

"You took a risk, even though you didn't know the outcome," I said, hoping my admiration came through the telephone connection.

"That's true," she said. "This was a big change for me."

With her work life heading in the right direction, Meghan tried online dating, only to discover how difficult it was to meet someone decent. She eventually met a man she liked. He was a teacher and a single parent like her. At first, he seemed interested in her, but his interest cooled within a few weeks of their first date. He talked about wanting Meghan as a friend and admitted he was dating another woman. Meghan didn't talk to him for several weeks.

One day he texted that he "missed her." He had stopped seeing the other woman. Yet even then, his intentions weren't clear. He told Meghan he wanted a friendship with her, whether or not a relationship between them developed. She couldn't tell if this meant he wanted to get to know her slowly or whether he had placed her in the friend zone for good. She felt completely out of control in this situation. Should she tell this man she would only spend time with him if he wanted to be romantically involved with her?

"How would he know whether he wants to have a relationship with you when he barely knows you?' I said. "How would you know that about him either?"

"I don't like not knowing what to do," Meghan said.

For several weeks, she felt so uncomfortable with the ambiguity of this relationship she considered just calling it quits. But she had a lot in common with this man. As a result, she decided to try a new strategy to help her cope with the discomfort of uncertainty.

"I remind myself I can't control the situation, and then I put it out of my mind," she said.

My mouth almost dropped open but turned into a smile.

"What a change," I said.

I thought about the Meghan I had met three years earlier: the firm grasp of her hand shaking mine, her white blouse fresh and unwrinkled on that hot summer day. She believed she knew exactly where she was going in life, and she had made a mental checklist to ensure she got there. This new version of Meghan was flexible, figuring things out as she went along. She was more relaxed and happier than she had ever been.

————————

Lisa called me in the winter of the second year of the pandemic for an appointment to discuss the latest problem with Greg, her now ex-husband. Her daughter recently got engaged, and Greg threw an elaborate engagement party for her. Of course, he did not invite Lisa.

"I was excluded from one of the happiest occasions in my daughter's life," she said. "That was so painful."

"I bet you would have been miserable even if he had invited you," I said.

"Probably. But he stole a moment of my daughter's happiness away from me. Greg always gets what he wants."

Then, as if the years hadn't passed, Lisa talked about whether she should have divorced him in the first place. Had she made a mistake? Maybe if she had waited longer, they could have worked something out. After all, according to what her kids told her, he doted on his new wife, the woman he had been having an affair with while he was married to Lisa.

"Why didn't he love me in this way?" she asked.

"That's exactly the point," I said. "He didn't act lovingly towards you. That's why you divorced him."

At first, I was worried about Lisa's backsliding. Then she made a statement that showed she understood her vulnerabilities more than I could see.

"I am not like this all the time," she said. "When Greg does something to trigger me, it puts me back to where I was when I first started therapy."

I was pleased at Lisa's insight into herself. Nonetheless, she needed me to bolster her self-confidence, and I did. "You are independent, capable, and stand up for yourself more than when I first met you," I said.

A therapist is partly a patient's cheerleader. I was hers, just as Joe had been mine when I divorced.

Besides the current problem with Greg, Lisa's life was going well. She had been involved with a man for three years, and this relationship differed from her marriage. When she married Greg, she never wanted to be apart from him; Lisa and her current partner led separate lives. She enjoyed her "alone time," as she called it. She liked being single and didn't want to get married again.

"That sounds like a great relationship," I said.

"I guess so," Lisa said. "I just wonder if this is love."

"What do you mean?" I asked.

"If I don't need to be with him all the time, does that mean I don't love him?"

I recalled her first therapy session, the shattered look in her eyes when she told me about her husband's affair. "You were so young when you met Greg. As far as you were concerned, the sun rose and set over him. You had no sense of who you were." I knew I was telling her the story of my marriage to Tom as much as I was describing her younger self. I took a quick breath. "After you divorced, you had a clearer sense of self. The fact you enjoy your time apart from your boyfriend doesn't diminish your feelings for him," I said.

"I like that," she said. "Getting divorced allowed me to develop a new self."

When Lisa's session ended, I picked up my pen to write her progress note. I commented on how well she was doing, predicting she would soon be ready to terminate therapy again. Then, as I often did during my decades as a psychotherapist, I thought about Joe.

I saw him weekly, and then biweekly, for the first two years after Tom left. Then years would lapse between appointments, and I would book a session when I couldn't solve a problem alone. Our last appointment had been eight years earlier, the year my son left for college. I was struggling with the adjustment to being an empty nester. We discussed finding a new purpose in life now my child-rearing days were over.

Towards the end of the session, I described my jumbled-up feelings: grief at my son going off on his own and pride at his success. Joe found the perfect words to capture my experience, as he had often done during the more than thirty years I had known him.

"It's bittersweet when your child grows up and leaves home," Joe said. "Just like when a patient terminates treatment." He stood up and hugged me goodbye, neither of us knowing he would retire at the start of the pandemic and I wouldn't see him again.

———

After I finished the teletherapy appointments with my patients for the day, I walked into the kitchen. Bob stood at the sink with delicate soap bubbles coating his hands. "I'll cook, you wash," I suggested early on in our marriage, and we have kept to that system for thirty-one years.

We decided to make our takeout Chinese dinner a special occasion: burgundy cloth on the dining room table, flickering candles, and glasses filled with red wine. We spread the contents of the little white cartons on our fancy china and dug in. After dinner, we stretched out on opposite ends of our olive-green, living room sofa. Maybe it was the many years I had spent as a therapy patient, but the couch turned out to be where Bob and I had our most personal discussions.

Sometimes, our conversations were close and intimate. We confided in one another about work problems, medical fears, money issues, or maybe conflict with our grown son. Other times, when we were angry, these talks were strained. The previous week we'd had one of these tense conversations when Bob joked about how obsessed I had become over a dress I bought for my son's upcoming wedding. I had asked him five times whether he thought it looked good on me.

"You are losing perspective," he said. "It's just a dress."

Of course, I knew that. I wanted him to understand the dress made me self-conscious about getting old and feeling unattractive. "That's why I keep talking about it," I said. "Teasing doesn't help. It hurts my feelings."

"Sorry. I won't do it again," he said.

When Bob and I argue, I like who I am. I look into his eyes, not off to the side. I'm not rude, but I don't mince words. My voice is clear, direct, and firm, so different from the timid, apologetic voice I used in my first marriage.

Divorce was a painful experience for me, just as it was for Lisa and Meghan. Yet, it became an unexpected opportunity, allowing us to leave behind an older version of ourselves and embrace a new one. None of us would have ever chosen divorce as a way to transform ourselves. Nonetheless, we were pleased with the women we became after we bounced back.

FURTHER RESOURCES

CHAPTER 1. LISA

Ephron, Nora. *Heartburn.* New York: Alfred A Knopf, 1983.

"Women in the Labor Force: A Databook." *BLS Reports,* April 2023, www.bls.gov/opub/reports/womens-databook/2022/home. htm#:~:text=The%20educational%20attainment%20of%20 women,with%2011.2%20percent%20in%201970.

"Percentage of the U.S. Population Who Have Completed Four Years of College or More From 1940 to 2022, by Gender." *Statista*, July 21, 2023, www.bls.gov/opub/reports/womens-databook/2022/ home.htm#:~:text=The%20educational%20attainment%20of%20 women,with%2011.2%20percent%20in%201970.

CHAPTER 3. MEGHAN

"New Study Shows That Millennial Women Live Life On Their Own Terms With An Impressively Pragmatic Approach." *Cision PR Newswire*, February 18, 2016, www.prnewswire.com/news-releases/ new-study-finds-that-millennial-women-live-life-on-their-own-terms-with-an-impressively-pragmatic-approach-300221992.

Hess, Cynthia et al. "Providing Unpaid Housework and Care Work in the United States: Uncovering Inequality." *Institute for Women's Policy Research,* January 2020, iwpr.org/wp-content/uploads/2020/01/IWPR-Providing-Unpaid-Household-and-Care-Work-in-the-United-States-Uncovering-Inequality.pdf.

CHAPTER 4. LISA

Lilienfeld, Scott O. and Arkowitz, Hal. "Are All Psychotherapies Created Equal?" *Scientific American,* September 1, 2012, www.scientificamerican.com/article/are-all-psychotherapies-created-equal/#:~:text=Although%20a%20number%20of%20commonly,few%20may%20even%20be%20harmful.

Nissen-Lie, Helene A. "Humility and Self-Doubt are the Hallmarks of a Good Therapist." *AEON*, February 5, 2020, https://aeon.co/ideas/humility-and-self-doubt-are-hallmarks-of-a-good-therapist.

CHAPTER 7. MEGHAN

Colino, Stacey. "Are You Catching Other People's Emotions?" *U.S. News,* January 20, 2016, health.usnews.com/health-news/health-wellness/articles/2016-01-20/are-you-catching-other-peoples-emotions.

Dickerson, Victoria. "Young Women Struggling for an Identity." *Family Process*, vol. 43, no. 3, August 9, 2004, onlinelibrary.wiley.com/doi/abs/10.1111/j.1545-5300.2004.00026.x.

Johnson, Sarah Lindstrom. "Future Orientation: A Construct for Adolescent Health and Well-Being." *International Journal of Adolescent Medical Health*, vol. 26, no. 4, 2013, www.ncbi.nlm.nih.gov/pmc/articles/PMC4827712/.

Wolfinger, Nicholas H. "Want to Avoid Divorce? Wait to Get Married, But Not Too Long." *Institute for Family Studies*, July 16, 2015, ifstudies.org/blog/want-to-avoid-divorce-wait-to-get-married-but-not-too-long/.

CHAPTER 8. LISA

Glass, Shirley. *Not "Just Friends": Rebuilding Trust and Recovering Your Sanity After Infidelity*. New York: Free Press, 2002.

CHAPTER 10. ELLEN

Lieberman, Matthew et al. "Putting Feelings into Words: Affect Labeling Disrupts Amygdala Activity." *Psychological Science,* vol 18, no. 5, May 2007, pubmed.ncbi.nlm.nih.gov/17576282/.

Lun, Janetta et al. "On Feeling Understood and Feeling Well: The Role of Interdependence." *Journal of Research in Personality*, vol. 24, no. 6, December 2008, www.sciencedirect.com/science/article/abs/pii/S0092656608000925.

Trafford, Abigail. *Crazy Time: Surviving Divorce and Building a New Life.* New York: Harper and Row, 1982.

CHAPTER 11. MEGHAN

"About Marriage and Family Therapists." *American Association for Marriage and Family Therapy*, www.aamft.org/About_AAMFT/About_Marriage_and_Family_Therapists.aspx#:~:text=Membership%20in%20the%20American%20Association,in%20a%20rapidly%20changing%20world.

Gottman, John. *Why Marriages Succeed or Fail: And How You Can Make Yours Last.* New York: Simon and Schuster, 1994.

Eisenberg, Nancy et al. "Parental Socialization of Emotion." *Psychological Inquiry,* vol. 9, no. 4, November 2009, www.ncbi.nlm.nih.gov/pmc/articles/PMC1513625/.

Damasio, Antonio. *Descartes Error: Emotion, Reason, and the Human Brain.* New York: Penguin Books, 2005.

CHAPTER 12. LISA

Gordon Julien, Jane. "Never Too Old to Hurt From Parent's Divorce." *New York Times*, April 21, 2016, www.nytimes.com/2016/04/24/fashion/weddings/never-too-old-to-hurt-from-parents-divorce.html.

CHAPTER 13. ELLEN

Miller, Harriet. "Behind the Rising Divorce Rates." *New York Times*, July 26, 1981, www.nytimes.com/1981/07/26/nyregion/behind-the-rising-divorce-rate.html.

Kennedy, Sheela and Ruggles, Steven. "Breaking Up is Hard to Count." *Demography*, vol. 31, no. 2, April 2014, www.ncbi.nlm.nih.gov/pmc/articles/PMC3972308/.

CHAPTER 14. ELLEN

Gaylin, Willard. *Feelings: Our Vital Signs.* New York: Harper and Row, 1979.

CHAPTER 15. LISA

"Women More Likely Than Men to Initiate Divorces, but Not Non-Marital Breakups." *American Sociological Association,* August 22, 2015, www.asnet.org/press-center/press-releases/ women-more-likely-men-initiate-divorces-not-non-marital-breakups.

Kay, Katty and Shipman, Claire. *The Confidence Code: The Science and Art of Self-Assurance – What Women Should Know.* New York: Harper Business, April 2018.

CHAPTER 17. ELLEN

Kegan, Robert. *The Evolving Self: Problem and Process in Human Development.* Cambridge: Harvard University Press, June 1982.

CHAPTER 18. MEGHAN

Gaspard, Terry. "Timing is Everything When it Comes to Marriage Counseling." *The Gottman Institute,* www.gottman.com/blog/ timing-is-everything-when-it-comes-to-marriage-counseling/.

CHAPTER 19. ELLEN

Ryan, Elizabeth. "Transforming Motherhood: Single Parent's Liberation in the 1970s." *Digital Commons @Wayne State,* January 1, 2015, digitalcommons.wayne.edu/cgi/viewcontent. cgi?article=2408&context=oa_dissertations.

Mattes, Jane. *Single Mothers by Choice: A Guidebook for Single Women Who Are Considering or Have Chosen Motherhood.* New York: Harmony, 1994.

CHAPTER 20. ELLEN

Kiley, Dan. *The Peter Pan Syndrome: Men Who Have Never Grown Up.* New York: Dodd Mead, 1983.

CHAPTER 21. MEGHAN

Hardy, James. "The History of Divorce Law in the United States." *History Cooperative,* May 29, 2015, historycooperative.org/ the-history-of-divorce-law-in-the-usa/.

Gilligan, Carol. *In a Different Voice.* Cambridge: Harvard University Press, 2016.

Lee, Catherine M. and Bax, Katherine A. "Children's Reaction to Parental Separation and Divorce." *Paediatrics and Child Health*, vol. 5, no. 4, May-June 2000, www.ncbi.nlm.nih.gov/pmc/articles/PMC2817796/.

CHAPTER 22. LISA

Jacobbi, Marianne. "The Power of Having a Great Role Model, Whether You Are 9 or 99." *Boston Globe*, January 18, 2022, www.bostonglobe.com/2022/01/18/magazine/ power-having-great-role-model-whether-youre-9-or-99/.

Carey, Benedict. "This Is Your Life (and How to Tell It)." *New York Times*, May 22, 2007, www.nytimes.com/2007/05/22/health/ psychology/22narr.html.

ACKNOWLEDGEMENTS

I want to express my gratitude to the two patients who allowed me to tell the story of their divorces; their generosity provided the inspiration for this book. A special thanks to "Joe" the therapist who helped me with my own journey of self-discovery during my divorce. Thanks also to Laurel Cohn whose skillful editing improved the book in ways I couldn't have imagined. Her wonderful editing is matched by her unfailing kindness.

I also want to acknowledge the contribution of the people I met in the Grub Street writing community. Michelle Seaton got this project off the ground, and Dorian Fox moved it along. Ashley Kalagian Blunt offered many insightful writing tips. Lacey Colligan and Evelyn Krache Morris read and commented on many drafts of this book. Marie Cahalane has been a wonderful friend, writing buddy, and constant cheerleader whose many invaluable suggestions helped me develop my work.

As the book neared completion, David Wogahn and Manon Wogahn offered advice on various publishing topics and designed a wonderful book cover. Thank you to both of them.

Finally, I am grateful for the support of my family. Benjamin Smith solved my technical problems and believed in my writing. Most of all, thank you to Bob Smith, whose perceptive insights improved my ideas and whose unwavering confidence in me kept me going until I finished the book.

ABOUT THE AUTHOR

E llen Holtzman earned a PsyD from the Massachusetts School of Professional Psychology, now known as William James College in Boston, MA. She has been practicing for thirty-five years and currently treats individuals and couples in her Boston suburban office. Her essays have appeared in *The Curve, Intima, Under the Gum Tree, Cognoscenti, Monitor on Psychology* and the anthology, *Same Time Next Week.*

www.ingramcontent.com/pod-product-compliance
Lightning Source LLC
Chambersburg PA
CBHW071152130626
46553CB00004B/1622